I0522690

Reckoning 4
Electronic Edition: Winter 2020
Poetry Editor: Danika Dinsmore
Fiction/Nonfiction Editor: Arkady Martine

Cover (and interior photos throughout):
Defense of the Environment by Didier Graves

Ornament:
Waterwheel by Commando Jugendstil

Reckoning Press
206 East Flint Street
Lake Orion, MI 48362
www.reckoning.press
ebook distributed by Weightless Books
printed by Book Mobile on 100% post-consumer recyled paper.

 ISSN 2474-7327
e-ISBN 978-0-9989252-7-1
ISBN 978-0-9989252-6-4

Reckoning 4

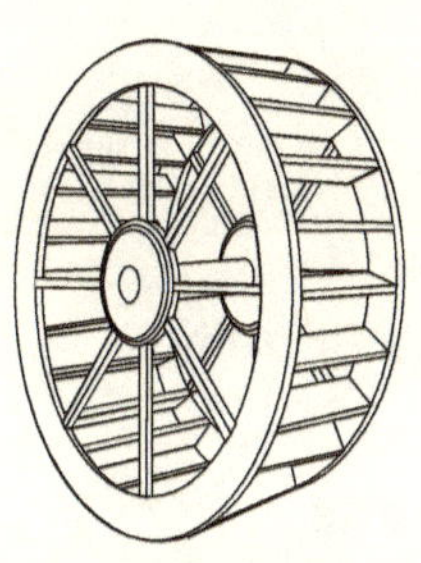

Cities

Contents

VIVANT

Cover (and interior photos throughout)
Defense of the Environment

Didier Graves

Didier Graves is a French photographer interested in 'social' photography in general and in social movements such as the 'gilets jaunes' movement that is currently shaking France.

From the Editors

Holding On When All That Is Solid Melts Into Air

Arkady Martine

I wrote this issue's call for submissions thinking of architecture. Thinking of drowned cities and burning ones, of sun-cracked concrete where the water can come in and fields gone too fast towards some warmer version of themselves, not even fallow any longer so much as *lost.* Of waiting for the next hurricane, on the twelfth floor of a Manhattan apartment building, thinking *well, we won't drown, but what's going to be left*—and of years later, watching wildfire trackers from a house in the high desert, wondering how fast, how far, how many dead.

I wrote the call with all of that grief on my tongue—I am a thing that loves cities and loves deserts and wants to lose nothing, and will lose anyway—and asked for *the point of contact where human alteration and ecological alteration touch; fantasias of density and of absence; blurs between organic and inorganic forms, places, and persons.* Asked for stories and essays that would think of architecture, of the built environment, and not merely write pain, but instead think of symbiosis, of touch, of memory. Of what could be built out of what has been built already.

The stories and essays in this volume of *Reckoning* are a gift to have received. They are anguished, vicious, exquisitely gorgeous; they speak, over and over again and in a thousand different ways, of *place*, of connection, of making and remaking. Of coming home, and never being able to come home again, and what you might do afterward.

The issue is dark, and it does hurt: but the world is, also. Dark, where it is not burning. And this is not a darkness of despair, or retreat, but one of recognition; a display of a wound, and a cautery—or a rope spun out in the dark, hand to hand, voices over the flood. It is an honor to share them with you.

Arkady Martine is a speculative fiction writer and, as Dr. AnnaLinden Weller, a historian of the Byzantine Empire and a city planner. Under both names she writes about border politics, narrative and rhetoric, risk communication, and the edges of the world. She is currently a policy advisor for the New Mexico Energy, Minerals, and Natural Resources Department, where she works on climate change mitigation, energy grid modernization, and resiliency planning. Her debut novel, *A Memory Called Empire*, released in March 2019 from Tor Books, has been nominated for the Hugo, Nebula and Locus Awards. Arkady grew up in New York City, and after some time in Turkey, Canada, Sweden, and Baltimore, lives in New Mexico with her wife, the author Vivian Shaw. Find Arkady online at www.arkadymartine.net or on Twitter as @ArkadyMartine.

The Dream of the Wood

Leah Bobet

the night of the windstorm
the city swayed

steel branches wrapped in old concrete

the leaves fall in strict equations:
material tolerance plus environmental
pressure plus the work of builders' hands.

in the morning, we count cracks:
birch lines in the drywall laid bare
for the deer. the corner panhandler lost
his hat in the night. *spare change, a nickel*
a quarter a dollar? I put palms to the sidewalk
and feel for roots, crouched, bent small,
parting rush-hour rivers of feet.

in the valley, the river wound round the birch, half in,
half out of water. the squirrels crept back to their nests
lean and loud, whistling as they gathered new twigs.
the muskrats drained burrows below, mirroring:
one crown wide, and one buried.

there are cracks in the city. we all feel it:
the thin drafts blowing through. in the wind,
I spread hands rootlike through the soil
and dream of changing: from our rusted degradation
point to tough green wood, flexed, bowed, unbreaking.

I can feel it coming, love, like the first
of spring: smoother, softer, here I go,
stretching hands-first into something
that bends, and then stands.

Leah Bobet's most recent novel, *An Inheritance of Ashes*, won the Sunburst, Copper Cylinder, and Prix Aurora Awards. Her short fiction has appeared in multiple Year's Best anthologies, and her poetry in *Uncanny Magazine*, *Goblin Fruit*, and *Strange Horizons*. She lives and works in Toronto, where she contributes to food security and civic engagement projects and makes heroic amounts of jam. Visit her at www.leahbobet.com.

Dead Horse Club

Jude Wetherell

> Barren Island is the only place or locality in or near the city of New York for the destruction of garbage and dead animals in the city, and is the only proper place for the rendering of the same. . . .
>
> —*The New York Supplement*, Volume 70 (*New York State Reporter* Vol. 104), containing the decisions of the Supreme and lower courts of record of New York State, permanent edition, May 23-July 11, 1901

The first horse makes itself from the bones of other horses scattered in the bay. It sews its parts together with the spines of baitfish. It drags itself from the water and bleaches on the island shore until it is pocked-white, picked clean as it can be by the flies and the birds and the mites that make caves of its marrow.

Still the first horse stinks. More than an ordinary corpse, more than the sweet rot at low tide, the pink undertongue of marshy sand. No one remembers that smell anymore. The diseased breath of the first horse fills the air now. It is the breath of the boiling tank, of bodies distilled to dust, fat-clogged sewers, the trash of the whole city rising in gas and embers to the sky. Even on the clearest, brightest day, out on the barrier of sand to the east where happy children play in the waves and their mothers pull their skirts up to their ankles, when the wind picks up there will be no forgetting the things that happen on this island. The first horse makes sure of this, most of all to the people who live here and cannot leave: the men who stir the tanks, the rag-picking women, the children whose sorry schoolhouse floods with the tide.

On the shore the first horse collects itself bone by bone. A diadem of jewels hangs over its hollow eyes. This is a treasure from a rag-picker, the loss of which earned a maid fifteen lashings in a fine house uptown when it tumbled out with the rubbish.

The first horse is used to taking things. It was born a whisper of breath from the mouth of a ship. It was cough and itch and boiling blood rolling far across this continent before the time came to collect the bones.

Yet the people of the island know the first horse by sight. Buckling with each step, it walks the streets of their town in the shadow of smokestacks, down the twisted lanes until it comes to the sunken schoolhouse. It pushes open the door with a nod of its caverned nose. The children feed it their fingers; it lets them lick its hollows in return. Beneath the tallow rot they taste something like freshwater and look up into its empty eyes with love.

The second horse never wanted to be, but here it goes: gathering itself out of baby shoes and broken glass, taking bottlemouths for eyes, the handles of meat cleavers for jawbones. Hairbrush bristles are the crooked line of its backbone; the second horse makes itself lopsided, one leg a stack of old boots, one a mantelpiece beaten to driftwood, one a collection of rolling pins, one a lady's dress twisted to a rope and stiff with saltwater.

The second horse is red, for it is holding itself together with clots of rust: the rust of doorknobs and window grates, the forks and knives and spoons of people who left their homes too quickly to carry them along. It is pulling itself from the water, bleeding its red hoofprints down the risen highways of the city.

The second horse knows it has a father. It is going to find him and crush his neck in its jaws of rotted wood. Dragging a rusty trail down the highway's median, taxicabs and trucks swerving, as it runs the second horse sheds the spoils of its father's war, a war waged on the people of the city. It releases and returns the guts of razed homes: ointments and treasures, brooms and soapboxes and nail polishes and crockery and Clorox bottles. From fire escapes and rooftops, stoops and storefront windows, people set down their work and stare. By the time the second horse finds its father it will have nothing left but rust and its boot-leather lips, drooling red spittle up the marble steps.

But with the highways its father has woven a labyrinth, and the second horse loses its way. Under the high sun, halfway down Long Island, it is peeling and flaking, and its glass eyes are burning prisms. By the side of the road a woman tending chickens runs to bring it water in a dirty tray. It stares at her strangely but stops to drink, in long rasping gulps.

When she pets its scaly neck, trying to understand, the second horse breaks to dust under her palm.

She takes up the scattered bottles and leaves them in her windowsills, and in the spring fills them with meadow flowers: Queen Anne's lace, milkweed, clover blossoms.

The third horse rises halfway from ocean slick, stretching its oily neck. Its skin is patterned with camera eyes, forever shifting, working muscles beneath of liquid mercury, bones of palladium and cadmium. Below the surface, swollen guts of polyethylene choke and stutter on hydrocarbon slurry, saltwater and antibiotic substrate. The third horse swims in this amnion, drinking it ceaselessly as the whales of old: its own blood and body. Nothing could ever be enough. The third horse was born famished.

It does not come ashore. The shores are further now than ever, and the city is quiet even in its highest towers.

The third horse did not fashion itself like its kindred but was beaten together in the surge of storms, a sticky nucleus snotting alive from ultraviolet radiation, a wet black foal dreaming beneath the waves. Now it drifts and starves, dreaming human dreams, its body an endless aching library, bloated with memory. Microprocessors and microplastics sway in its intestinal dark. The third horse knows a hundred billion names, murmurs ten trillion histories to an audience of plankton evolved to eat its quiet secretions. It knows so much and still it hungers.

When on occasion a ship passes the third horse—a tanker buoyant and empty, a girl-sized woman paddling a skiff—it will roll its heavy head in that direction, and blinking camera-eyes with no recognition, dive again below to suck poison through its teeth.

One morning the girl-sized woman paddles out with a knife and an empty jar; on the far-away shore they need fuel, and the third horse's blood will do, in a pinch. Clots of it have washed up on the beaches, and in their campfires and cookstoves it makes a strange multihued flame that smells sharp and strange, but it burns, and this is what matters. Now from her skiff she spots it like a storm in the water, spinning with its own gravity. As its current draws her closer, she murmurs thanks for the gift of its blood as she has been taught, her own voice startling her. It is small but sounds so loud, with all that endless water around her, the empty towers sparkling in the distance.

An oar's-length away the third horse raises one eye to the white spot of the sun. Gently, her skiff drifts onto the dark halo it makes in the water. Its head is lolled at the sky, showing its neck, and she almost laughs. She has only to reach her knife into that outstretched vein and muscle, and what will fill her jar will feed many fires, and many mouths on shore.

She takes the knife and the jar from her belt, subtle as she knows, and reaches.

The moment before she is pulled under, she sees a face reflected in its shiny hide—hers—before her world overturns and all is dark and plugged and choking. It has swallowed her, is eating her whole with gnashing thrusts of a huge tongue, or claws, or unseeable teeth, nothing certain but the force of its hunger. She yearns to scream but cannot speak, to struggle but cannot move, and the harder she tries the more it tightens its chokehold, until she has gone totally still, and the third horse goes still around her. Then she feels nothing at all.

Until she opens her eyes and sees at once the whole horizon, the skeletal city in the distance, the sea extending everywhere, the sky embered bright with stars. When she stirs in the water and heavy droplets fling from her mane, she is surprised, but distantly. She knows so much more now, and she is rearranging her molecules, summoning her parasites, swimming for the shore, changing the waters with her as she goes.

The fourth horse has been here from the beginning. It is bone-meal, glass ground to sand, metallic flakes, polymer and hydrocarbon dust.

Mostly it is air. It rises from our firepit, shimmering pale silver, bucking on the wind. Here it is small, but the fourth horse can make itself out of anything it likes, anything that remains. We see it some nights, dancing over the bloody-bruised sunsets and violet-shadowed storm heads; when the rains come the fourth horse trips high into the clouds, where it scatters and rearranges and scatters itself again.

One day soon it will go higher. It will gather the rime of the sea and the ash of our fires and it will rise hot and fast, hooves forging solid in the heat of its ascent, hurling itself through the darkening layers of the sky.

And it will not stop. The fourth horse knows what stars are made of, because we told it.

When it comes home again, we will not be here to greet it, but until the last of us lays in the earth we will look to the heavens and remember.

Jude Wetherell lives in Flatbush, Brooklyn, New York, and is a 2015 graduate of Clarion West. Jude's work has previously appeared in *Luna Station Quarterly* and *The Wild Hunt*. Twitter: @jmcwwww

Two Tides

Anna Kate Blair

We stand above the water when we stand at the water's edge. The foreshore is elevated, offering protection against hurricanes that come with harvest moons. Williamsburg began with rowboats, and then came steamboats, and then a bridge, and then many forms of forgetting about the river.

Recently, we started to remember.

Williamsburg is not the Brooklyn that most people inhabit, but it's the Brooklyn that most people talk about, the Brooklyn that has become an international brand. Before I moved to New York, I knew this neighbourhood's narrative, that it had once been an industrial centre, and then a place where artists lived and worked, squatting in lofts, and that now tourists often spent a day there, returning to their homes to tell their friends that they went to Brooklyn, that they saw more than just Manhattan, and that it was really quite nice. I, too, once visited Williamsburg as a tourist, sampled artisanal chocolate and giggled at a neon sign outside an underwear store reading "LOVE, LUST, PANTIES."

It is not only tourists talking about this part of Brooklyn, though. Sometimes it feels as if everybody in New York is at once complaining about Williamsburg and dreaming about Williamsburg. I myself have spent an hour on the subway travelling from my home in another Brooklyn neighbourhood, Sunset Park, and arrived with notebook and camera to look at a place that seems to slip through my fingers, more famous than understood. Williamsburg is a place with an outsized significance, like a bellwether for the twenty-first century. It is a microcosm of the larger city.

The world is changing, and Williamsburg is changing first.

Williamsburg was once a major manufacturing hub, an industrial centre considered a rival to Wall Street. Pfizer Pharmaceuticals and Standard Oil had factories and refineries here. Domino Sugar's factory is still standing, one of the last signs of those industrial decades, but it's being converted into condominiums. After World War II, the role industry played in the life of the city changed, and factories fell vacant; jobs disappeared. In the 1980s and 1990s, rents in Manhattan began to increase and artists moved across the bridge, to Williamsburg.

The city has rezoned Williamsburg three times in the twenty-first century under the pressures of development. The City Council prioritized waterfront access and low- to mid-rise housing in 2002; Mayor Bloomberg presided over a major rezoning in 2005 that rendered the factories closest to the waterfront residential; and in 2009, the city tried again, attempting to correct the excesses of 2005, with a new zoning plan that claims to protect the character of certain inland streets by requiring that they remain residential and by creating height limits for new construction.

It may have been too late, or it may have provided the wrong incentives; Williamsburg is disappearing under scaffolding, replaced by computerised renderings of an anodyne future.

I attend a panel discussion, organised by Open House New York, that contemplates what we might learn from Williamsburg. Gregory Wessner, the organisation's Executive Director, suggests that the changes taking place in this neighbourhood have "nothing to do with New York City," but spring instead from changes in the way things are made today. Leah Archibald, Executive Director of Evergreen, claims the problem is money. In the last rezoning, the government agreed to create a twenty million dollar fund for manufacturing, but deposited money in it slowly, reaching only half of the promised total. Archibald's job focuses on assisting working-class businesses in Williamsburg, trying to help these businesses find financing and navigate regulatory issues, and also in trying to get public acknowledgement of their continued presence.

"We probably lose a little more than we win," she says.

There is no discussion, here, about the tide. We are not thinking about Williamsburg as the edge of Long Island, as a fortified coast. Access to the water was a reason that Williamsburg became an industrial center, and it's a reason, now, that people want to live here. This is short-term thinking, because this neighbourhood will be submerged.

The waterfront was evacuated in 2012, when Hurricane Sandy struck. People taped up their windows and bought alcohol and snacks, caught taxis to hotels in Manhattan. The water rose above the shoreline, and sandbags sealed the entrances to towers. Further inland, too, there were flooded streets.

Another storm could turn Williamsburg into a peninsula and Greenpoint, just north, into a small archipelago. The tides are always getting higher.

Williamsburg's rezoning was intended to promote affordable housing, but instead created an influx of luxury units, the most jarring of which are the towers clustered beside the pier for the East River Ferry. These are all glassy and forgettable, taken individually. These are non-places, bearing no trace or memory of what was before. They have no history. They have no connection to the earth. They have names like "THE EDGE."

It could be anywhere in the world, perhaps, save for the Chrysler Building across the water. Those who live in Williamsburg and work in Manhattan—most of those living in these towers—have an enviable commute, boarding the ferry and jetting across to Midtown or south to the Financial District. This is one of the most expensive neighbourhoods in New York City, which some people find hard to believe because Brooklyn, until Williamsburg, was the place where people moved when they couldn't afford Manhattan. But you could go weeks, living here, without setting foot on a Brooklyn street.

There are benefits to building and living in towers. In theory, dense living frees up land for parkland and agriculture, meaning food can be produced and transported efficiently. In theory, these towers could relieve pressure on the market for apartments. But in

Williamsburg, they don't. Their main effect is to create a hard barrier between Brooklyn and the river, with only small paths between them for people to permeate.

I close my eyes outside a bar on Bedford Avenue and the crowds of people laughing, chattering over one another, sound almost like gulls calling out as they scavenge for food. I imagine animals that might replace people in the waterfront condominiums, picture birds perched on fifteenth floor balconies, lizards on the mezzanine, fish swimming up from the basement and over lobby tiles.

If we think of neighbourhoods for people in the same way that we think of ecosystems for animals, we remember that we don't just need homes, but also jobs that suit us nearby, and food, too, that we can access and afford. Our conversations about gentrification often focus on affordable housing, but when applications for one such scheme in Greenpoint, just north of Williamsburg, closed recently, over half the applicants were rejected because they didn't make enough money to rent the units. Developers speak of creating jobs, but the jobs they create aren't the jobs that people want: hotels where there once were foundries.

I don't know which species are, or will be, native to this habitat. I don't know to whom Williamsburg belongs. The histories are obscured; the futures are uncertain.

Opposite the Brooklyn Brewery is the Wythe Hotel. "Everybody knows the Wythe Hotel," says a woman with curly hair, as I stand on the street looking at a map. It's in Wallpaper*'s guide to New York City. "The Wythe has given Brooklyn the grown-up hotel it deserves," reads the guidebook.

"I don't know if *grown-up* is the right adjective," my companion says, looking at the crowd outside. I'm not sure about *deserves*.

The Wythe Hotel is a very busy place, with guests and visitors to the bar and restaurant constantly moving through the lobby and elevators. The staff are preparing for a wedding party later in the day. There are signs in a corner to direct visitors to the Northern Innovation Happy Hour. In the basement's private dining room, I see a copy of Forbes's '500' issue lying atop a stack of boxes.

The Wythe Hotel used to be a barrel factory. There were still people working here when Morris Adjmi Architects were invited to work on the building's conversion into a hotel. Jeremy Reed, giving us a tour of the hotel, points out the many features the architects chose to keep—the tracks in the ceiling, the details around the doors—and those they changed. The floors can hold a lot of weight, Reed tells us, because they're made for heavy industry.

It's a decadent hotel, in more ways than one. The owners, reportedly, were not concerned about making a profit, and the financial crisis bought Reed and his team the luxury of time to finesse their design before any construction took place. There's a rooftop bar, where a cocktail called Brooklyn View costs $18: visitors look out across construction and warehouses, dusty lots, and the Brooklyn Brewery.

In the guest room, the focus is not on Williamsburg, but on Manhattan. The architects kept three of the building's original façades, but cut off a bay on the building's western side and replaced it with glass, differentiating the façade facing Manhattan from the others. In the guest room on the southwest corner, exposed brick obscures Brooklyn; glass, from floor to ceiling, directs the eye out of the hotel and beyond low-lying warehouses, west across the East River, to the city's skyline.

The design is nice, and the architect is friendly, and perhaps the Wythe Hotel wouldn't have felt quite so cruel in 2006, before Williamsburg fully became the place it is today. Reed tells us that the owner, looking for furniture, walked around the neighbourhood until he found somebody making beds, and then commissioned a prototype. The bed we see is beautiful, made of wood with rope stitching around the frame that suggests an old-fashioned box-spring. I wonder if the woodworker is still based in Williamsburg.

"These logos are all taken from companies that don't exist anymore, to add authenticity," says Reed, directing our eyes further down, to a brick wall opposite a lower floor.

On the evening Hurricane Sandy hit New York, in September of 2012, high tide was at 8:46 PM. The tide, that day, was not much higher than any day that year, but was accompanied by a nine-foot storm surge and high winds.

Kinfolk is less than a block from the Wythe Hotel, and it used to be a garage. Now it's a coffee shop and a clothing store and a bar, with space for live music and other events. There's a sign outside the clothing store reading "I spent half my money on liquor and fancy t-shirts. The other half . . . I wasted."

John Berg, the architect who designed the interior, is meeting groups of visitors outside the entrance to the bar. The client told him that they wanted something that felt like it was designed by "an off-the-grid hippie mathematician from the Pacific Northwest," and that caught his attention. Williamsburg has almost no trees and none of the dramatic coastline of the Pacific Northwest, but rather an artificial waterfront under which we've lost the real one. This neighbourhood is on every grid—even the streets line up as a grid. I am taken by the coolness of the concrete and the way the light filters down through the ceiling, made with Douglas firs from Washington State, but it must take an incredible lack of self-awareness to ask, in Williamsburg, for a design along these lines.

If you come on a Friday or Saturday night, Berg tells us, there are huge crowds of people and, outside, "a line of cabs to take you back to Manhattan."

When Hurricane Sandy struck, some Williamsburg residents disobeyed the order to evacuate and stayed to watch, making their way to the forbidden waterfront. Some leaned against the winds on the pier, while police tape waved in the air behind them, and others held empty plastic bags up to the sky, holding the handles and attempting flight.

The water is a playground and a threat.

"As an architect," Peter Zuspan says, "preservationists are my nemeses."

We are in a room that Zuspan designed, a performance space with black lines crossing patterned white aluminium panels at a range of angles, disappearing into the dark voids that form doors and a recessed balcony. This room is at the centre of National Sawdust, a non-profit music venue in a brick building, once a sawdust factory.

The capital that allows National Sawdust to operate came from rising property prices, with a model in which investors own the building. The metal components in the sleek central room were made locally, though the manufacturer has since moved elsewhere in the borough. The neighbourhood's development, here, has been leveraged to benefit local artists and local industries.

It feels impossible, in Williamsburg, to be pure in ideological commitments, to keep one's place without allying oneself with the financial forces that are driving change. I think of the imaginative commitments of art and music as at odds with capitalism's value systems. I think of architecture and design as fields with social commitments, as arts which aim to solve problems and create affordable solutions that work for everyone, and I forget that, for some, art and design are business opportunities, part of a process of creating products that sell.

It could be water that breaks the system, that resists in a way that people cannot. Water, already, is pushing at Williamsburg's infrastructure. It will be necessary, soon, to close the tunnel through which the L Train, the neighbourhood's main subway line, runs, in order to repair the damage caused by Hurricane Sandy. It only takes a tiny amount of rain, less than a quarter of an inch, before sewage tanks overflow, sending waste into Newtown Creek, just north of

Williamsburg. We saw the hurricane as an anomaly, as an event, but the emergency is continuous, invisible to those looking elsewhere.

A few blocks south, at FACE Design and Fabrication, a woman in a floral dress is talking passionately, to a man who doesn't seem impressed, about how she thinks "the community needs to see makers," about how she's trying to get spaces for industrial fabricators that people can visit, close to green spaces. Reuben, working in the next room, tells me they're worried developers will notice them if the community does. It's a noble intention, he suggests, to encourage general awareness that manufacturing is still taking place in Williamsburg, and isn't just a thing of the past—but what if developers see another opportunity and come after the block they're working on?

"I hope we can stay here," Reuben says. FACE were pushed out of the East Village, and then the Meatpacking District, and then moved to another site in Williamsburg, on which condominiums now stand. The William Vale Hotel is close, and very visible, and Reuben tells us another hotel is going up beside it. I notice a sign reading "FOR LEASE" on a building across the road.

There are so many predators, ready to pounce.

In the evening, during the hurricane, after hours of sirens and loudspeakers urging evacuation, after the wind and rain had combined to scare everybody from the pier, after Williamsburg's streets had filled with water, there were still people by the waterfront, watching, as the Con Ed Substation across the river exploded and lower Manhattan lost power. In a video taken that night, a crowd on a corner are illuminated by the explosion; they are silhouettes in raincoats surrounded by shimmering water. I think of Guy Debord's idea of spectacle as something larger than people, something that people watch and absorb, silently, without forming a critical commentary. There is silence, for a moment, and then there is shock, exhilaration, voices saying "woah," "fuck," and, to the person holding the camera, "did you get that?"

We are thinking, in architecture, about how to disappear. We do not presume, now, that our buildings will last hundreds of years. We don't think about buildings that will last forever, but celebrate the temporary, predict dilapidation, imagine surfaces wearing thin, structures breaking down entirely. It is wasteful; it is exciting.

Industry, of course, is not innocent either.

In 1978, a streak of oil appeared in Newtown Creek, and over fifty acres of soil is still contaminated today. On a map showing where chemical and petroleum spills have occurred, Williamsburg is covered in dots. There are brownfields and superfund sites everywhere.

We did not know, in the late nineteenth and early twentieth century, about the larger consequences of oil. We did not expect hurricanes or floods. We are nostalgic, now, for a flourishing industrial centre that we could not accept today. Williamsburg has always been tipping toward crisis.

In many places, contaminated soils overlap with floodplains. Nine months after Hurricane Sandy, samples showed that contamination from industrial areas had migrated to residential ones.

I suppose the basements will not fill with fish after all.

Across New York, the areas that flooded during Hurricane Sandy are being watched by developers. Red Hook, further south, was evacuated entirely, with water reaching seven feet on some buildings. Over a year later, businesses were still closed for repair. The city hasn't yet invested in work to mitigate the effects of similar events that will occur in future, but there is a complex for tech companies under construction, and 45,000 apartments being planned. The waterfront warehouses of Sunset Park, where I live, are in the first evacuation zone, and developers are currently campaigning to bring a hotel to one of them. Their dream, it seems, is to make the neighbourhood like Williamsburg.

The only exception thus far to this desire to build where the water went is in Oakwood Beach on Staten Island, where the city has started buying houses that were damaged in the hurricane and returning them to nature, transforming the neighbourhood in a strategy of managed retreat. There are wild turkey and deer where once there were harried commuters and high school students.

There are many buildings in Williamsburg that used to be something else. Diviera Drive, which I walk past as I return to the subway station, was once a garage; it's now a bar and an Italian restaurant with a boat named "El Dorado" decorating the yard. I don't know, yet, if it floats.[1]

Architecture, across this neighbourhood, is being used as a means of creating links with the past, an attempt at reconciling the changes taking place with the place itself. Everybody wants to move to Williamsburg, but as they move to Williamsburg, Williamsburg disappears.

The dust from construction makes me thirsty.

It will all, one day, wash away.

1. Diviera Drive has since closed.

Anna Kate Blair is a writer and architectural historian from New Zealand. She has had work in publications including *Litro*, *The Appendix*, *King's Review*, *Antithesis Journal* and *10 Stories: Writing About Architecture*.

Damned Water

Brigit A. Truex

> "Reservoirs created by the [Hydro Quebec] James Bay Project cover an area of 12,241 square kilometers, the largest bodies of water created by humankind."
>
> —*from the* James Bay Road website

your power needs water
traced to distant points of light like stars

unreachable   foreign
reflected in the fragile bones of quick-
silvered fish   drowned caribou   the snow-pale geese

relatives that feed me
decaying within as the fine root-web tangles in
the absence of water

siphoned and malign
feeding insatiable turbines
hulked on your layered landscape
a new topography shoveled and scraped

trembling beneath the weight
of your vast new lakes   never measured to memory
nor washed blue   on faded maps

here, where treeless spaces
crackle with a grid of
black and fire

all this to bring distant points
            their light like stars

A mixed heritage of Canadian First Nations (Cree/Abenaki), French and Irish as well as her natural surroundings influence the poetry of Brigit Truex. After a dozen years in California's Sierra Nevada foothills, she has settled in the bluegrass plateau of central Kentucky. That variety of viewpoints is clear in her varied writings.

Current and future publishing credits include international journals and anthologies such as *Locked Horn Journal*, *Vallum*, *Yellow Medicine Review*, *Contemporary Literary Review India*, *Canary* and *apt*.

Truex is the author of four chapbooks. She was also finalist for both the Locked Horn Prize and the Hopper Prize. Her latest book, *Sierra Silk*, is available from Amazon.

The Last Good Time to Be Alive

Waverly SM

@antediluvian: london isn't alive, zuri
@antediluvian: london is just a city. it can't hurt you.
@ZRI_: yeah yeah i know
@ZRI_: just let me be delusional for a minute okay i'm having a Time over here
@antediluvian: can you get here? are the railways still up?
@ZRI_: lmao no
@ZRI_: power's off and everything
@ZRI_: it's whatever. it be like this sometimes
@antediluvian: i love you
@antediluvian: okay? i love you. don't fucking die in rugby.
@ZRI_: dude
@antediluvian: without wanting to steal your look or whatever
@antediluvian: just let me be delusional for a minute okay
@ZRI_: you lunatic
@ZRI_: i love you too.

London isn't alive, says Marlo, but that's easy to say from her place inside its heart. You don't think babies conceive of—anything, really, before they're born. But you can't imagine you thought of your mother as alive when you were taking up space in her body way back when. Outside of the city, on the wrong side of the flood barrier that hasn't been opened in years, it is easier to see it for the monster it is. It sucks the life from the land around it, and then shrugs off the consequences when they threaten to hit home.

The rain has not stopped falling. It's the middle of the day at the height of summer; the windows are slick with condensation, the air heavy with humidity and heat. When you were a little girl your mother would watch downpours like this from the window and mutter darkly to herself: "It never used to be like this."

You go about the process of preparing for the flood like you are only a machine, some switch flicked inside you to turn off all but the essential. Mains power off. Generator unplugged. Sandbags at the doors—you trap the tight curls of your hair under the hood of your raincoat, shove the hems of your jeans down into your boots. The water's already halfway up the garden. You've been lucky in the past; it's made it this far and no further, the godawful reek of the brook behind your parents' house lingering in the air long after the flood had receded. But this is the future, and the clouds overhead are smog-choked and steely grey, and the endless thrumming of rain on rooftops is shutting down pathways in your brain. It isn't going to stop. When you get back inside, there's rainwater, inexplicably, soaked right through your socks to your feet.

There's no sound in the house but the rain—no refrigerator humming, no air conditioning unit keeping up an endless desperate wheeze. You don't remember the last time you felt small here, like the vastness of home could swallow you whole.

@ZRI_: Hey mama

@ZRI_: I just wanted to let you know I'm taking care of the house

@ZRI_: The whole place is sandbagged now and I turned off the power

@ZRI_: How are things in London?

There's no reply.

@ZRI_: i'm looking out at the street and the kid i used to babysit is chucking toys out the window

@ZRI_: like trying to see if they'll float? i think?? is the reasoning there???

@ZRI_: made me think of yr old video about the car trying to drive through a flood

@antediluvian: !! what old memes can tell us about flooding!

@antediluvian: is it awful that i still think the original vid is kind of funny

@ZRI_: nah it's fine

@ZRI_: gotta laugh, right?

@antediluvian: we used to be better at that

@antediluvian: like someone saw this person doing this incredibly stupid thing and got his phone out to film it

@antediluvian: the whole time telling the driver what a fuckin tit he

was being
@ZRI_: what a bellend
@ZRI_: what a fuckin knobhead!!!
@antediluvian: and then he shared it on the internet bc it was funny! it just was
@antediluvian: like obviously people still absolutely live to humiliate other people on line or whatever but i don't think the car flood video would happen now
@ZRI_: idk
@ZRI_: i'd be filming amal's toy purge rn except it'd eat right into my battery life
@antediluvian: idk if people would laugh
@antediluvian: i think they might just find it sad
@antediluvian: like this is what we do for fun now......... we just throw toys in the flood water. hashtag good old days hashtag bring back hanging.
@ZRI_: lmao
@antediluvian: idk maybe i'm just a big sensitive Baby
@ZRI_: no i don't think so
@ZRI_: you're human
@ZRI_: more historians should be human about this shit imo
@antediluvian: 'historian'
@ZRI_: car video is history okay!!! you talk about history
@ZRI_: i want to watch your flood meme doc now. fuck
@antediluvian: battery?
@ZRI_: ye
@ZRI_: listen
@ZRI_: if phone signal goes
@antediluvian: zuri no
@ZRI_: you know it could happen and if it does i want you to check in on my mum and dad
@ZRI_: they're in the ez motel in stratford under the name christopher emmanuel
@ZRI_: i know it floods out there and mum's not replying to my messages
@antediluvian: i'll do what i can
@antediluvian: but for real though
@antediluvian: i need you to not talk like you're going to drown or something

@ZRI_: that's okay i can do that
@ZRI_: that was like my one thing. we good now baby i promise
@antediluvian: lmao 'baby'
@ZRI_: wish i could watch the flood documentary
@ZRI_: any of your videos really
@ZRI_: kind of just want to hear your voice? today in gay as shit with zuri dot online
@antediluvian: god
@antediluvian: i love you extremely
@antediluvian: and when this is all over you're fucking. coming to london and we're watching the video together
@ZRI_: yes'm
@ZRI_: <3

It's your thing, the vintage heart emoji, the one that looks like a less-than-three. Marlo did a whole documentary once on that, the way people made faces and expressions out of numbers and punctuation. Before people even had emoji. Sometimes you want to burst into song about Marlo—*my girlfriend is an internet celebrity and she knows so much cool shit,* the single, the album, the musical—except that nobody in Rugby has the time or the wherewithal to care. There aren't any famous people here. Just warehouses and terraces and the ruin of an old cement works, looming large over every skyline in town.

You're the person you are because you lived here all your life. Your parents got you into high school and promptly disappeared to London, living out of bunk beds in a motel room because it worked out cheaper than commuting to work by train. Every time you see them, they're a little more like strangers, in their second-hand suits with ID cards on lanyards around their necks. London devours all the life it absorbs, bit by bit. You could swear your dad is shrinking to fit the room he lives in, harder at the edges every time you say goodbye.

You stayed, though. You studied. You got used to filling silences in your parents' tired old house, blasting witchhouse and blurcore on speakers you rigged up yourself, falling asleep to video footage of Marlo explaining how things used to be. You are tough and enterprising and equipped for disaster. You are Zuri goddamn Emmanuel, wringing out your socks over the bathroom sink, eyes straining for perspective in the unlit dark. You live here and no goddamn flood is going to change that now.

The garden's underwater, out back. You pitch up in the living room instead, looking onto the street as the drains start to choke. There's a plastic toy boat bobbing weakly in a puddle that is threatening, not without grounds, to turn into a lake.

@antediluvian: <3

Before Marlo even knew who you were, you had learned the ending of her goddamn flood documentary by heart. *What does this tell us about the way things used to be?* she asked, as the picture faded from a flooded suburban street to a photograph of historic London, gleaming in the sun, the Eye still unbranded on the skyline. *At first glance, there's not a whole lot to learn from a silly video from way back in 2016. But I think it tells us a lot about how people in the tens understood the world they were living in—a world that was starting to see real-time evidence of its own impending doom. We didn't know how to come to terms with it, so we laughed at it, as best we could. We looked past the unthinkable for something we could understand—which was comedy, or absurdity, or just plain old human error. We didn't know how to answer for everything we'd done wrong. Can you blame us? Could anyone?*

You snap a quick photo of the boat. You'll send it to Marlo later, when the power's back on. Once it's safe to laugh in the face of death again.

This is the best time to be alive, said Marlo; you remember how your heart swelled in your chest, watching her film herself walking through the city, watching her expressionless face open up into a smile. London all around her, the perfect co-star, bright and enticing and undrowned. *Maybe this is the last good time to be alive. We don't know what's coming next, or when it's coming. Of course that's scary, and of course we should pay attention. But maybe we should be readier to look for joy, as well. Do we want to look back from the end of the world and realise we wasted the last days we had?*

Maybe you should throw all your shit out the window, too. Amal from two doors down looked like he was having fun.

You give up on the ground floor at about 5pm.

It's still light outside, which is something. You can sit in your parents' bedroom, its every surface coated in a thin film of dust, and watch the world descend into chaos with something like a bird's eye view. A half-eaten tub of ice-cream in your lap, scavenged from the freezer and already melting at speed. Water's rushing down the slope of the street toward your house like the worst kind of waterfall, some unnatural wonder of the world. If you close your eyes, you can almost hear it seeping into the walls and the floorboards, soaking the bones of the house so they'll never get dry.

@ZRI_: mama if you are reading this could you please message back

@ZRI_: I don't have power to check the news and i want to know if you are safe

Your parents won't care about the house. It's barely theirs anymore. They would have sold it years ago if you'd been able to sleep in a store cupboard at school, like a really dutiful daughter would've done. Mostly they'll be mad about the water damage, although it's not like there's anyone to blame. You did everything you could. Your hands are shaking in your lap, too unsteady for a decent grip on your phone. You're so fucking frightened you could puke.

@ZRI_: downstairs just flooded lol

@antediluvian: well fuck

@antediluvian: tell me you're upstairs

@ZRI_: yeah, with food

@ZRI_: we had ice cream in the freezer can you believe it

@ZRI_: be a crime to let it melt

@antediluvian: i hate this so much

@ZRI_: yeah i'm not exactly hype about it myself

@antediluvian: you have to leave

@ZRI_: little late for that babe

@antediluvian: no i mean after this. it is not safe for you to be in the suburbs anymore

@ZRI_: rugby's barely a suburb

@ZRI_: a freight terminal maybe

@antediluvian: come live with me

The world drops away, precipitous, leaves you suspended like some dumbass cartoon character in the air. You've visited Marlo's place. It's some high-rise shit in Tower Hamlets, gentrified almost to death thanks to a comparatively minimal flood risk and paid for entirely with internet video money. She does well out of what she does; it's a really nice flat. You just see Essex underwater in your head every time you look out the window. Barriers closed, water rising downstream. You have a ticket to safety, ready and waiting whenever you want it—but not Amal, not his mum. Not any of your neighbours, who will be digging out their emergency kits right about now if they have any sense about them.

What sucks beyond belief is that the thought has its hooks in your heart. No more water seeping under the door. She caught you at the best possible time.

@ZRI_: whoa
@ZRI_: are you asking me to move in with you
@ZRI_: i mean i've heard of shipping but this is pretty intense
@antediluvian: u-hauling!! oh my god zuri it's called u-hauling
@antediluvian: shipping is
@antediluvian: whatever
@antediluvian: not the point. come live with me. i'm central and high up and insured
@antediluvian: the flood barrier works in my favour and i need it to work in yours too
@ZRI_: marlo
@antediluvian: no listen i am trying to be sincere for once in my life can you just
@ZRI_: i know
@antediluvian: let me do that
@ZRI_: i promise i'm not trying to be an asshole i just like
@ZRI_: i don't think i can just quit
@antediluvian: 'quit'
@ZRI_: on home.
@antediluvian: the same home you just called a freight terminal
@ZRI_: idk what to tell you
@ZRI_: sometimes home is garbage
@ZRI_: doesn't make it any less home
@antediluvian: zuri i cannot go through this again okay
@antediluvian: i'm not physically equipped to be alive and in love with you and know you're right in the middle of a flood and not know from minute to minute if i'm ever going to hear from you again
@antediluvian: and i know this sounds like the most entitled bullshit
@antediluvian: i know this is scarier for you than for me
@antediluvian: but i am scared, zuri
@antediluvian: i don't think i'm great at being scared

You don't realise you're crying until there are big, rainbow-smeared blotches of water on the screen of your phone. It's fine. You scrub at your eyes with the back of one hand, swallow your tears until your breathing's started to calm. You want to be with Marlo. You don't know who you are without your home wrapped tight around you. You're a crab inside a shell, and if you leave that shell then you'll turn into something you don't know how to be, laid bare before the elements with nowhere to hide. But you want Marlo, more than anything in the disintegrating ruin of the world. You want Marlo's safe place, high above the water where catastrophe can't get you. If there's a flood barrier, and you know in your heart that there'll always be a flood barrier somewhere, then there's a miserable, craven part of you that needs to be on the right side.

There's no Brighton anymore, no Essex, no Kent. London closed the barriers and it left them behind to drown. How long does Rugby have, if it keeps getting worse, if the tides keep rising and the rain keeps falling all your life?

@ZRI_: me neither

@ZRI_: can we talk about this later? like i know you're worried and i get it and everything but

@ZRI_: i am also scared and i need to concentrate on like

@ZRI_: not, being that,

@ZRI_: so i don't completely lose my whole shit,

@antediluvian: that's okay

@antediluvian: i'm sorry. i love you.

@ZRI_: i love you too

@ZRI_: and you know i want to be near you

@antediluvian: i do

@antediluvian: it's okay, zuri. i promise it's okay.

@ZRI_: i don't want you to be scared marlo

@antediluvian: hey. if i'm not great at being scared then maybe it follows that i am great at being brave?

@antediluvian: so i'm going to test that theory

@antediluvian: and maybe you can do the same and we can compare notes later

@ZRI_: <3

@ZRI_: can you like

@ZRI_: keep your phone on you

@antediluvian: like i haven't been physically attached to it literally all day
@ZRI_: lol that's fair
@antediluvian: <3
@antediluvian: i'm here.
@antediluvian: i'm not going away.

The light gives up before the rain. Sunset happens all at once; the clouds swell and darken and blot out the sky, and just like that, there's nothing to see. You get on your knees and dig out the emergency kit from under your parents' bed—wind-up torch, bottled water, tinned fruit and tuna and beans enough for a couple of days without power. It's not a small box. The last time you had to use it, you were new in high school and your parents had just left town. You got under the bed with the torch and a book and you tried to forget that you were twelve, and alone, and with no guarantee that anyone would find you if you drowned.

Not tonight. You resume your post at the window like you're a cop in a prison watchtower, like actually the water is trapped in here with you. You're eighteen years old and so you turn the torchlight onto the street, where the water is almost at window height and rising. If there's anyone else at their windows looking out, then they'll see. You might be going down, but at least one person is going to know that you were here.

For a split second, you don't think anything of the splash.

What gets you is the sounds that come after, these weird, choked-off little gasps and shouts that hesitate right at the edge of your hearing. You pause, and you listen, and you nudge the window ajar, and it takes you a second to make out what's going on—it's Amal, it's the kid from down the street, his dark head bobbing just above the surface of the flood. The light from your torch hits a little speck of plastic, just out of his reach and floating ever further away.

You don't even have to flip the switch. All your inessential processes start to power down on their own; your body knows what needs to happen next.

@ZRI_: marlo i gotta go for a minute

@ZRI_: <3

You drop your phone onto your parents' bed and you hurtle down, torch in hand, two stairs at a time. The hallway's flooded up to the second step—up to your knees, pouring right over the tops of your rain boots and soaking your feet in an instant. It doesn't matter. The grossness of it passes you by. You tuck your hair up into the hood of your coat, zip it right up to your chin and pull the drawstrings tight. You open the front door and you're kicked in the shins by a tsunami puked up from the overburdened drains, but that doesn't matter, either. It can't matter, because there's a three-year-old baby out there in the water, and nobody that small can swim well enough to handle a flood.

You force the door shut behind you, and you take a breath of air that reeks of shit, and you throw all your weight against the current.

There's nothing left in the world but the wind and the rain, plastering your hood to your hair and your sleeves to your skin. It's *cold*; you hadn't expected that, which is almost impressive for being so stupid. Middle of summer or not, the world is cold like this, with water up to your waist and soaking you all the way through. You drag yourself through the flood, through the confusion of cold and dark, and onto the pavement, shouting all the while: "Amal, holy shit, Amal, can you hear me?"

Your voice is so fucking small, and the rain and the wind are drowning you out—drowning you, full stop, no qualification required. Your face is numb, freezing, except for where the cold has made it a bright bloom of pain. You keep moving forward, down what would be the street if you could see where the fuck you're going. You try again—"*Amal*"—but your mouth isn't working right; you're slurring a little where your lips have gotten too cold, muscle memory not quite enough to get you by.

He doesn't see you. He doesn't even turn his head, intent on that fucking toy where it bobs just out of his reach. It doesn't matter. You feel it like a knife in the gut when he falls, *splash*, gone under the surface—like a wire in your head being cut, instantaneous, leaving you paralysed and useless in the dark.

He doesn't scream when his head breaks the surface, or when it dips below and out of sight again. He just *reaches,* up and out of the water like he's trying to find purchase on the sky.

You wrench yourself, hard, back together. You take a step, and another, and you keep going and you keep reaching until you can grab him and lift him clear of the flood. He's so heavy it hurts to hold him up, but he's *alive*, breathing, clinging to you and sobbing terrible breathless sobs into your coat. You should comfort him. It's so dark and so cold and the rain is lashing at your body like it's trying to fight you for him, and you know what you should say but the words stick hard in your throat. You don't have it in you to string together a sentence. You barely have it in you to go back, following the current, back to the window he found his way through, where his mother is screaming his name into the night.

With the last strength you have, you lift him up up up and into her arms. She clutches him close, dripping wet and reeking, crying hard enough that her whole body shakes. He's the only family she has, this kid you used to babysit while she worked late shifts at her second job. For a second there's no storm, no flood. There's just a mum holding her son, who survived.

You go. The door opens easily when you reach it, pushes back hard when you try to close it again. You make it, you figure, maybe halfway up the stairs—just clear of the water, whatever that means—before you drop. Your hands are wet and filthy and shaking on the fastenings of your coat, on the soles of your boots, your socks and your shirt and your bra and—everything. It's all ruined, isn't it? You peel away layer after layer, trying to get clean, and you don't realise you're crying until there's nothing left to claw away but your skin.

It's so fucking stupid, is the thing. There's a bath towel upstairs, maybe more than one. You could use some of the bottled water, try to get yourself clean, except your whole body is trembling and useless, and you're crying hard enough that it hurts to open your eyes. This isn't you. You are Zuri goddamn Emmanuel and you *deal* with shit; you don't cry about it, a huddle of raw nerves and bare flesh that couldn't even make it up the stairs.

It's so stupid. The world is ending. You're living in the end times and the most you can do, the absolute outer limit of your capacity to help, is rescue one kid from a flood. He nearly drowned, he *definitely* inhaled a whole mess of filthy water in the process, and you didn't even think to fetch the toy he went in to save. You can't open the barriers on the Thames, or force London to accept its share of the things the world's done wrong; you can't repair the holes in the ozone, take planes out of the sky, burn all the poison out of the ocean or the air. You're one person. It's bigger than you, all of it. The house is going to flood no matter what you do, over and over until it finally drowns.

Boneless, hopeless, the stink of the flood choking you by degrees. That's you. It always has been. It's not enough to try to be better, anymore.

@antediluvian: zuri what
@antediluvian: what do you mean what are you doing
@antediluvian: if you don't reply right this second zuri i swear to god
@antediluvian: come on come on come on
@antediluvian: ZURI
@antediluvian: oh my god what did you do
@antediluvian: where are you
@antediluvian: i'm losing my fucking mind

Your fingertips are wrinkled and tender but they are dry, and they are clean. You cradle the phone in your hands, huddled on your parents' bed and swamped in a dressing-gown you co-opted from your mum, and wait to feel worse than you already feel. It doesn't happen. Maybe you've plateaued. You climbed the whole mountain, and from the peak of feeling terrible, you can see a whole world of terrible things, sprawling endlessly away from you in every direction.

@ZRI_: i'm so sorry
@ZRI_: i'm okay i'm here
@antediluvian: i am so fucking mad at you
@ZRI_: yeah i
@antediluvian: i am going to physically come to rugby and fight you
@ZRI_: probably deserve that
@antediluvian: god
@antediluvian: zuri i am
@antediluvian: in the immortal words of the ancestors
@antediluvian: crying irl
@antediluvian: you could have fucking died

@antediluvian: i wouldn't even have known
@ZRI_: i know
@ZRI_: i'm really sorry
@ZRI_: i know it was stupid i just
@ZRI_: the kid was drowning
@antediluvian: what
@ZRI_: the kid
@ZRI_: he was throwing his toys
@ZRI_: he got out the downstairs window and i saw him and i just
@ZRI_: i couldn't
@antediluvian: holy shit is he safe??
@ZRI_: yeah
@antediluvian: jesus
@ZRI_: he was just trying to get one of his toys back
@ZRI_: i couldnt even find it for him marlo
@ZRI_: he was crying so much
@antediluvian: zuri
@antediluvian: you're like
@antediluvian: i can't believe
@antediluvian: i love you so fucking much zuri i wish i were there i wish you were here
@antediluvian: idk how to do this anymore
@ZRI_: lmao me neither

Or maybe you haven't plateaued. Perhaps you are just hiding from it all, burrowed down deep inside the crab-shell of your body, waiting for the sadness to crest overhead. It might break itself apart against you but you won't even feel it where you are. It can be something that happens, for once, to somebody else.

@ZRI_: if i come to london
@ZRI_: could you really like
@ZRI_: is there actually room in your flat or were you just
@antediluvian: yes
@ZRI_: trying to get me to agree or something
@antediluvian: zuri
@antediluvian: there's room
@antediluvian: i promise
@ZRI_: i feel weird inviting myself to live with you lmao
@ZRI_: hey there, minor internet celebrity, it is i, your new and surprising housemate

@antediluvian: no
@antediluvian: you didn't invite yourself
@antediluvian: i invited you and i would fucking love it if you accepted the invitation
@antediluvian: more than anything in the world
@ZRI_: haha well okay then i
@ZRI_: i guess i accept
@antediluvian: when the water's gone down we will talk trains
@antediluvian: okay? i will make it work and that is a promise
@ZRI_: i fully do not doubt it
@ZRI_: @ flood waters watch yourselves marlo is ready to part the sea
@antediluvian: hell yeah baby
@antediluvian: i'm gonna get you directly out of there come hell and/or high water
@antediluvian: preferably and, tbh
@antediluvian: i could take em both
@ZRI_: i believe it
@ZRI_: and i love you
@ZRI_: <3
@antediluvian: <3

The rain's starting to slow—not stop, but it's something. It'll do, short-term. You're sitting up in bed and you're drifting, Marlo's last little less-than-three heart blurring at the edges as you start to lose focus; your whole body is heavy with exhaustion, your skin tender where you scrubbed it clean of the flood. You think *floating* for a moment, and then you unthink it, pull yourself back before you float into a current you can't swim against. You're drifting. Like a bird on an updraft of wind, high above the water and the world.

Your phone buzzes in your hands, once and again and again. The vibration in your palm pulls you back into reality, three sharp jerks of a chain.

@GlorisEmmanuel: Hi sweetie sorry I forgot to charge my phone!! Lol
@GlorisEmmanuel: No flooding here praise God! Ur papa and I stayed home all day watching modern lovers can u believe they had a video maker on lol! Like your friend marlo tho her videos were all about pranks haha

@GlorisEmmanuel: Love u sweetie ur papa says hello!!

You don't register your own reaction until your knees are pressing hard against your forehead, your shoulders shaking with useless, breathless laughter. There has to be something to leaven these last remaining days, some small, stupid joy you can cling to. Marlo will laugh as well, you think, when you can show her at last in the flesh.

Waverly SM is a speculative fiction writer preoccupied with apocalypses, impossible choices, and the ambient trauma of living in the world. They're a 2019 Lambda Literary Fellow and have been mentored, as part of a cohort of emerging LGBTQ+ voices, by Benjamin Alire Saenz. Waverly studied English at Newnham College, Cambridge; since then, their work has appeared in Argot Magazine, and will appear in *Stim: An Autism Anthology* (Unbound, forthcoming). They can currently be found trying to approximate the anchorite lifestyle in Oxford.

Resource Extraction Zone

Lissa Harris

> Sometimes I live in the country
> Sometimes I live in town
> Sometimes I have a great notion
> To jump into the river and drown
>
> —Leadbelly, "Goodnight Irene"

It's been nine years since the last 500-year flood, which means we're due for another one in five or ten. Climate change math: the only thing you know for sure is that the numbers are always the wrong order of magnitude.

In the last flood, Irene, I never saw a drop of water. I was high and dry in a second-floor apartment in a neighborhood that got lucky, running an experiment called Let's Do Local News on the Internet, which had everybody around here pretty skeptical 'til whole towns started washing away. Overnight, the idea of finding out what was happening before the paper came out next Wednesday began to look a lot more attractive. We spun up a 24-hour live blog, tracked washed-out roads and lists of the missing, and did our damnedest to let the rest of the clueless world know how badly our region had been shattered.

Two hours from civilization, and we might as well have been on the moon. On the Brian Lehrer morning news show, where they patched me in to talk about Prattsville being gone, they were bitching about the subway not running.

The flood before that, in 1996, didn't have a name. It was freakish warm rain on top of three feet of January snow, and it liquefied the valley. The Batavia Kill behind our house became a sea. We got candles and flashlights, waited for the power to go out, and watched our neighbor's chest freezer roll end over end through the hay field. I was home from college, and I had pinkeye, so in lieu of more exciting recovery work, they set me to ironing page after page of irreplaceable hand-written ledgers rescued from rising waters at the Margaretville Telephone Company, which kept the locations of all the phone poles.

When the next one hits, I want to be ready, so here I am. It's September, the bank of the East Branch is heavy with goldenrods and asters, and the night air is still warm enough to be heady. One guy yells out to be careful, the river's undercutting the bank where they mean to put the strainer into the water. Maybe they'd better find another spot. *No,* I shout, *I can get down there!* and scramble down the slick bank like a lizard, along with one of the few other women here. *We got it! Hand it down to us!* we yell.

I'm brand new on the fire department, I know what none of these parts and valves are called or how they work, and I'm fizzing with the joy of being useful.

The strainer, when it is handed down, proves to be a big perforated tube of steel, locked onto the end of the hose that feeds up the bank and into the chrome-and-glory fire truck waiting above. Heavy as the thing is, the current wants to bend the stiff hose and press the strainer back toward the bank, where it scrapes and bumps in the rocky shallows. We feed it into a deeper eddy, chock it in place with a rock. Useful, by God. Maybe I belong here.

Already a gorgeous monster, the truck is even more magnificent in the green and humid dark, floodlit in triumphant white. When the pump goes on, it makes a huge, thrilling, vibratory sound, the unmistakable sound of important men doing important things. Dials and gauges tremble. The third lieutenant is in charge of running the pump, and he squints at a red LED number display dithering along to the roar of the engine. He's trying to bring the water pressure up to where the chief wants it. Somewhere in the night, on the other end of the mess of hoses and valves wending through the grass of the riverbank, between the overhanging trees and across Route 28, the water we're pumping out of the river is leaping in a pretty parabola over the sewer treatment plant. The plant hasn't caught fire, thank God. We're doing our annual flow test, for practice, in case it ever does.

That's the city's water flowing through our hoses. The city's sewer plant too, run on the city's tax dollars, to protect the city's nine million from the perpetual peril of our shit.

It's New York City, of course. There isn't any other city in the world; surely none worth mentioning. We say "the city," because to say the whole and proper name makes you sound like a tacky fake cowboy in a commercial for salsa, and to say "New York," like New

Yorkers do, is to cede ground that belongs to us, too. We *are* New Yorkers.

That feels like a technicality, though, a sop to the politically irrelevant. Something Andrew Cuomo might say into a big foam cartoon microphone. So instead, maybe we'll say we're from Delaware County, as if that meant anything to anybody; there are too many Delawares just like there are too many New Yorks. We're from Margaretville, population 560 and falling. We're from the Catskills, a dark, inchoate place, with no clear boundaries. We're *upstate*.

Never mind where we are. If you don't know the place, it won't mean anything to you. That's why people come here, if they weren't here already. To be nowhere, to get away, to taste that pure elixir.

The water is all the city's. All the water there is: the river, the wet squelch of the grass, the puddles in potholes, the music of rain rolling off the roof of my old house and landing with a hollow ball-bearing *blong* on the propane tank in the yard. The land around here for miles is a wrinkled tarp with the Pepacton Reservoir weighing down the bottom of it. 140 billion gallons full to the brim, the Pepacton is the largest and the clearest of the six that filled up the old valleys long ago, and every drop that rolls downhill toward it is spoken for.

Of course the city made it. Of course they did. Only 15 years before the moon landing, and every bit as much of an engineering marvel. People remember; that scab isn't fully healed yet. They bought what they could, condemned what they couldn't, moved the graves and dammed up the whole valley. They're still here. Their lawyers write our laws. They buy more and more of our land every year just so it can lie fallow, so cows won't shit on it and people won't build on it. So when it floods, like it does more and more often these days, all that washes down into the reservoirs is trees and rocks and mud, not cars and oil tanks and prizewinning Percherons and the entire contents of the local CVS pharmacy department. The city occupies us. They have their own upstate police force. Where did you think your goddamn water comes from?

In a descendant of the watershed, a full-throated disquisition on this topic is never far beneath the surface.

I have never witnessed anyone deliberately pissing off the

Shavertown bridge into the Pepacton, but surely some son of the valley with the blood of drowned Arena in his veins makes a regular religion of it. Never mind. Worse things ended up in there during Irene. The solution to pollution is dilution.

The city is far, far larger than its maps. Beyond the five boroughs' borders, beyond the thousandfold glittering points of light, beyond the listening ear of the last cell phone tower, lies the resource extraction zone. The poorer we become, the more valuable we are.

The city never stops buying land in the watershed. Year after year, there goes another old farm, another back forty sold off to the DEP. If the city ever stopped buying, the state Department of Health and the federal EPA would force them to build a water purification plant they can't afford. But ask a local, and you'll hear the inexorable logic of the paranoiac whose enemies are all too real: the city wants us gone. They're trying to starve us out, a slow economic war of attrition. Squeeze our towns down into the narrow river valleys, so the floods that grow more wrathful with every generation can sweep them away. Endgame: Depopulation.

Mention any of this to a visiting downstater and watch their brow furrow with confusion. No one wants that. As a topic of concern to your average New Yorker, "people are living in your water supply" doesn't even crack top ten.

They don't have to want it. The ecological law of colonization requires no intent. Apply pressure on a critical resource. Watch it eat away at the community, little by little. Shift a variable, watch the landscape change.

Climate change will have winners and losers. The warming world will want more water. We have all we could ever need here, if we can manage to keep from starving, or drowning.

We are all under siege as the world warms: rising seas, rising rivers. The city has a $20 billion resiliency plan, overseen by a growing Office of Climate Policy and Programs. We have the volunteer fire department. Like the village it serves, it's smaller and grayer than it was.

We drain the hoses and pack up the gear, which is just as much work as setting up for the flow test, and involves more slugs. Me and the other new guy on the department, we're learning how to work as a pair to uncouple the big ring valves that plumb the hoses into the trucks, one of us holding the heavy metal coupling while the other whales away at it with a mallet. We're not very good at it at first. We're getting better.

If I can hack basic fire training, I'll learn to do swift water rescues. Those who can probably should. At 43, I'm one of the younger ones. It's long since time I stepped up to volunteer.

When the next flood hits, no one is coming for us.

Unlikely but stubborn ruralite, prone to nerdery and gleeful belligerence. Lissa Harris is a writer, editor, swordfighter, and seventh-generation Delaware County resident. Along with her wife, Julia Reischel, she was founding editor of the Watershed Post, an independent digital news outlet that covered the rural Catskills from 2011-2017. On Twitter too much at @lissaharris, or on Tinyletter at EmpireOfDirt.

The Wall and the Water

E. M. Wright

The wall looms outside Amanda's window, its overlapping concrete segments curving into the distance like a vast serpent. It rises to the height of a four-story building and stretches to the north and south until it merges with the horizon. Three years ago when she first arrived at the refugee camp, before the water came, she couldn't stop touching the wall. Nobody touches the wall anymore. The water's too deep now, but at the beginning she and the other refugees pressed against the wall as if their longing could bore a hole through it. Several times a day she leaned her forehead against the pebbled concrete and listened to what sounded like the quiver of a thousand hearts imprisoned inside the wall, but was only the wind rustling in the salt marsh that used to surround the camp. The refugee camp is not a place for listening to hearts, hers or anyone else's. Every time she touched the wall she felt herself shrink into someone harder and smaller. Because of her daughter, Tiana, she stopped touching the wall. She taught herself to look at the water and sky instead, but in her dreams the wall abrades her cheeks and drips with the tears she doesn't cry when she's awake.

Today for the first time in many months she looks at the wall. In an hour she'll meet with the camp commander for a re-entry review. The last time a refugee was approved for re-entry was thirteen months ago. It's a day when she needs to be as impervious to hope as a pebble. A crusted border of silver salt ripples across the wall just above the water line. She licks her chapped lips. In the shadow of the wall the water looks purple, like the skin of a plum. Tiana's seven years old and has never felt a ripe plum split open beneath her teeth. Sorrow curls around Amanda's tongue, then slides down her throat, lodging in the fluttering tissue of her lungs.

Four feet below her the water laps dark and hungry at the side of the dormitory. The cot frame creaks as Tiana crawls over and lays her head on Amanda's thigh. Since the water rose, forcing residents to double up in the small dorm rooms, Amanda and Tiana have been sharing one narrow cot. She pulls Tiana's thumb out of her mouth, then laces her fingers into Tiana's small, damp ones.

"Momma." Tiana's chin digs into Amanda's thigh. "Don't look at the wall."

The wall undulates under Amanda's fixed gaze. It's an optical illusion that their roommate, Layla, has told her about. Stare at the wall long enough and it starts to pulsate like a breathing animal. She imagines it writhing away into the water, imagines the water rushing into the space where the wall stood, spreading across the land to find a river that can return it to where it belongs. Tiana's hands on her face turn her away from the wall.

"Tell me a story," Tiana says. She pats Amanda's cheeks, the urgency of her touch so near to a slap. "Tell me about the water. Tell me about how it's going to wash away the wall."

Long before their arrival at the camp, the ocean began nibbling the marsh that encircled the refugee compound, but five months ago it stopped nibbling and gulped. Two inches of amber water like under-brewed Lipton's tea seeped out of the ground overnight. In the morning ground that had been only spongy and damp before revealed itself as glassy and opaque beneath the rising sun. The smell of ozone, like lightning, filled the air, rising off the water. Since then the water's grown steadily deeper.

She touches the tangled, salty loops of Tiana's hair. "Today isn't a day for stories."

"Under the water everything's more beautiful," Tiana prompts her. "Tell me about the kelp forests and the fish playing hide and seek."

Every night Tiana swims through Amanda's dreams, backstroking through a midnight expanse of water and sky, diving into pools of starlight, seaweed entwined in her hair. Every night Amanda clings to the wall. Slender ghost sharks, dark veins pulsing beneath their pale skin, nudge her legs in a languid invitation as she presses herself against the wall. Every night Tiana smiles as she slips beneath the water to join the sharks, disappearing into the depths of the ocean. Night after night Amanda wakes with the taste of saltwater on her lips and a throat raw with suppressed tears.

She's relieved when the door opens, jarring the side of the cot where she and Tiana sit. In the hours since breakfast, Layla's managed to find fingernail polish. Her glossy fuchsia nails gleam against the chipped paint on the doorframe.

"You're not dressed." Layla frowns at Amanda's jeans. "I told you to borrow my dress."

Layla has a knack for camp life. Illicit rations of cooking oil keep her face and hands soft. Her purse bulges with fistfuls of butterscotch candies and packs of spearmint gum. When the most recent platoon of soldiers started their tour of duty a few months ago they brought boxes of donated clothing. Layla plucked a silky, flowered sundress, store tags still attached, from the piles of plaid blazers and pilled sweaters. Because it was Layla, none of the other women challenged her right to claim it.

"Won't fit me," Amanda says. The seat of her jeans is almost worn through, but they're hers from before. When she bought them, her life hadn't yet cracked apart, split by the fissure that swallowed the dusty earth of her home.

"Oh, stop." Layla grabs the dress from a box beneath her cot and drapes it around Amanda. Pink hydrangeas bloom on a creamy background. Cool silk slides across her bare arms. Tiana crawls into her lap and lays her cheek against a cluster of hydrangeas.

"You belong on the other side of the wall," Layla says. "You deserve to be there."

"None of us belong." Her voice grates like the cries of the gulls that roost on the dormitory roof. "We're the leftovers, the ones they don't know what to do with. We'll be here until the water covers us, washing our bones clean."

Layla lifts Tiana from Amanda's lap. "Honey, go find some of the other kids."

The sharp angles of Tiana's elbows and the fragility of her neck evoke the long-legged egrets that bobbed through the marsh before the water rose; beautiful creatures that alit in Amanda's life, then disappeared too soon. When Tiana leaves the room without looking back at her, it feels like water rising over her head.

Layla settles onto the cot next to Amanda. "Soon they'll have to let us all in, whether or not our applications are approved. They won't keep us here. Have a little faith."

"Faith in what? Humanity?" Amanda leans out the window and inhales until salt coats the inside of her mouth with the regretful, unripe taste of green olives. Above the water the stucco corner of the building is already crumbling. This is a building with light switches in rooms without light fixtures, electrical outlets that fizz with sparks, and floors that slant to meet the walls at drunken angles. Everything about it betrays its hasty construction by the lowest bidder.

"Yeah, humanity." Layla loops her arms around Amanda. "What else is there for us to believe in?"

Little in Amanda's life has encouraged her to believe that relying on the good will of others is a sound survival strategy, but the yeasty warmth of Layla's body pressed against her back makes her want to try.

"A little hope won't kill you." Layla's hand on her cheek turns her away from the window.

She lets herself rest her head on Layla's shoulder. "You really think they're going to approve all of us for re-entry?" she asks, eyes closed so she can't see the wall.

An hour later the flowered dress swirls around her legs as she climbs out the window that's become a door. When the water first started to rise, the soldiers bolted metal walkways to the sides of the buildings just below the second-story windows, joining the dormitories and headquarters together with a safe, dry path. Now the water has crept over the walkways.

She holds the window frame for balance as she steps into the water. For a moment its buoyancy resists her weight. When she was Tiana's age she spent a summer watching Jesus bugs skate across the pond behind her foster family's house. Every time she steps into the water, its hypersalinity encourages a sharp instant of belief that this time she will skim untouched across the surface, just like the Jesus bugs of her childhood. She cannot rid herself of the painful irrationality of hope.

The water closes over her foot and creeps up her ankle. The commander will tell her that her application has been approved. Or he'll tell her it doesn't matter—he's taking everyone to the other side of the wall because the water has risen too high. Or the rising water will float everyone over the wall like a theme park ride, the kind that comes with life jackets and a safety guarantee. The water is only water, the wall only a surmountable obstacle. She and Tiana will find a life on the other side of the wall, emerging from this place unscathed, as if it never happened.

She splashes through the water. At the other end of the walkway she climbs through the window to emerge in the officers' mess hall. They, too, have been forced to double up and repurpose rooms as the water has risen. A few security officers seated around a folding table in the middle of the room glance up, then return to their card game. The damp hem of the dress wilts against her legs.

"Commander's that way," one of them says, hooking a thumb toward the back of the room.

She finds the camp commander in a small room off the mess hall. It might once have been a supply closet, but now it's an office. When she knocks on the open door, he rises into a polite crouch beneath the sloping ceiling. She recognizes him as the officer who smokes cigarettes on the headquarters dock at dawn.

"Call me Jake," he says as he shakes her hand. His shirt cuff rides up to display the salt rash on his wrist.

She holds his hand a little too long, grips it a little too tightly. "Was my application approved?"

"Have a seat," he says.

He's still standing, his knees bent and his shoulders stooped to accommodate the low ceiling. His crew-cut bristles like the sea urchins that cluster beneath the docks. Her knees bump his desk as she sits in the rusted folding chair. What does it matter whether he's friendly or not? The decision on her application has already been made by someone on the other side of the wall, someone who can't see the sun blisters on her daughter's legs, someone who doesn't care that Tiana knows flowers only as a pattern on a hand-me-down dress and has never tasted a plum.

"It's better if you just tell me. This is my seventh re-entry application."

The skin around his eyes looks soft and bruised. He folds himself into his chair like his joints hurt, but she can't feel sorry for a man who has the right to leave this place.

"Please just tell me," she says, but she already knows. She rubs her fingers across the dress, tries to remember Layla's warmth and certainty, but even Layla hasn't managed to talk anyone into taking her to the other side of the wall.

"You know, there are a lot of complicating factors for refugee re-entry." He opens the file and touches the letter on top. "A lot of records were destroyed."

She reaches across the desk and takes the letter from him. "We regret to inform you" it begins. She makes her eyes scan across the page so that it will look like she's reading it, but the words have dissolved into indecipherable black marks. The damp paper curves into waves beneath her fingers.

"You can re-apply," he says. Dark, untrimmed hair lines the insides of his nostrils. He touches the papers on his desk with broad, nicotine-yellow fingertips. "Form F-9V12 lets you request—"

"A comprehensive review by a citizens committee. I know. I've submitted that form before. Twice."

Sometimes it would be easier to believe that there's nothing on the other side of the wall, that the refugees and the soldiers that guard them are the only people left in the world, but then every three months the USS North slips across the waves and a new platoon of soldiers steps off still smelling of hamburgers and gasoline. The way they stare at the wall and the endless water tells her that the world she used to know still exists in places, it's just that she's no longer a part of it.

"You can't keep us here. The water's still rising."

A plain silver band encircles his ring finger. Somewhere on the other side of the wall there's a person he loves. The knowledge makes him seem approachable, as if all she needs to do is find the right words to make him understand.

"There's so few of us left here. What could it matter if you took us back with you? How are a handful of women and children a threat to anyone?"

"The US doesn't have unlimited resources. Times are hard for everyone. We have to make sure that the people in our country have a right to be there." He taps the file in front of him. "You don't have birth certificates for you or your daughter." He says it kindly, but the message is clear. He's a rule follower and she doesn't fit his rules.

"Everything of mine is missing. The places I've lived, the place where my daughter was born—they don't exist anymore." The town where she gave birth to Tiana was one of the first to disappear into the earth. She saw pictures on the news of the jagged chasm where the hospital used to be, the air thick with dust.

"You've provided no contact information for any established citizens who can sponsor you. Nobody's come forward to corroborate your application."

"It's always just been Tiana and me." Layla's the closest she's come to having family in a long time. "Resubmit the application as it is. No changes. I have nothing to add."

Jake reaches for the ink pad and stamp at the corner of his desk. The creases of his shirt are wilting in the damp air. He rolls the stamp in red ink, presses it to the top page of her application, then holds up the paper so she can see that he's stamped it "urgent."

"It's the best I can do," he says.

"My daughter's been at this camp for almost half of her life. Tiana's seven. Her whole life is in a single building. And the water keeps rising." Her belief in the possibility of him ushering everyone in the camp onto the deck of the supply boat is so strong that it feels like a memory of something that's already happened. She can see herself sitting on the deck, Tiana at her side, the boat churning along in the lee of the wall until they come to a place where there's no more wall.

Jake thumps his stamp in the red ink again and inks the duplicate copy of her application. "I have a daughter, too. Emily. She's four years old."

She imagines a preschooler with his long jaw and thick eyebrows, living the life she'd wanted for her own daughter. "You could take us all with you at the end of your rotation. Every person in this camp. Load us onto your troop ship and drop us off on the other side of the wall."

"Look, there are problems on the other side of the wall, too." His voice is gentle. "The storms are bad everywhere. There are worse places than this camp, you know. At least here you're fed. Looked after. At taxpayer expense."

Salt burns her foot where her wet sneaker has chafed the skin. Even in this windowless closet, she can feel the looming presence of the wall. When Jake's rotation ends in a few months, he'll wear the same unconscious look of relief on his face that all the soldiers do when they leave. She closes her eyes to help herself remember how to talk to someone who has the right to leave this place, but the wall is there behind her eyelids.

When she opens her eyes, Jake's wrestling with a desk drawer swollen in its frame. He takes out a chocolate bar wrapped in foil and pushes it across the desk toward her.

"Here," he says, "for your daughter."

She doesn't want it. How many chocolate bars will he hand out so that he can travel home at the end of his tour of duty and kiss his wife and daughter, believing that he's a good person?

"Go on, take it." He tosses the chocolate bar into her lap.

If she's nice enough, maybe he'll change his mind. She hates the part of herself that believes this might be true, the part of herself that's afraid to be angry. "My daughter loves chocolate," she says. "Thank you."

"Mine too," he says. She can see that he believes in her gratitude. The floor rocks, as if the building is shifting on its foundation. A pen slides across his desk and he catches it before it falls to the floor.

"Nothing to worry about," he says. "Just a little subsidence."

She puts the chocolate into her pocket. It's only a few ounces, but it weights her steps as she leaves his office, reminding her of all the things she can't give her daughter: ice cream cones and playgrounds, air that doesn't taste of salt, a future. Her legs feel almost too heavy to lift her over the windowsill and into the water.

Clusters of bivalves encrust the sides of the ramp. A trace of algae furs the metal panels beneath her feet. Quarter-sized jellyfish float in the dark water, trailing poisonous tentacles. The wall looms above her. High tide is still half an hour away, but already the water covers the tide line on the wall.

After the water swallowed the first floor of the refugees' dormitory with its common area and kitchen facilities, the soldiers knocked out the walls between three bedrooms on the second floor. It's a place to feel less alone. Even though her borrowed dress is soaked to mid-thigh, Amanda goes there instead of her bedroom.

The sound of Layla's voice floats through the open window. Amanda climbs out onto the dock that runs the length of the building. On the ocean side of the dormitory the wall's just a shadow unless you crane your neck to see it rising into the sky above the dormitory. Layla's telling a story to some of the other women, hands gesturing. Their laughter blends with the squalling of the birds wheeling above them. None of them notice Amanda standing by the window.

Tiana's alone at the other end of the dock, stretched out on her belly. As Amanda walks over, Tiana wriggles forward, cantilevering herself over the water. She's humming the lullaby that Amanda sang her to sleep with when she was a baby. The water creeps up her wrists to her elbows, then higher. Amanda watches the water engulf Tiana's arms. A school of silver fish no bigger than a thumbnail eddies around the dock like chain mail flashing in the sunlight, then disappears beneath. Tiana lowers her face until the water touches her lips. Her hair floats in mermaid tendrils on the surface of the water.

"Don't," Amanda says, her voice squeezed thin with fear. The air tastes like tears.

"Look, Momma." Tiana touches a barnacle clinging beneath the water line. It closes at her touch, tightening into a gray rosebud. "It's pretty, isn't it?"

The words release Amanda from her paralysis. She falls to her knees and snatches Tiana into her arms. "It's not pretty," she says before she slaps her hard enough to leave a white handprint across her cheek.

It's the first time she's ever hit her daughter.

Startled tears turn Tiana's eyes glassy. Her fingers drip seawater onto her shirt as she puts her thumb in her mouth.

"It's not pretty," Amanda repeats. The second time she hits Tiana she's had time to think about what she's doing and she does it anyway. The second time she hits her it's because even the sting of her hand on her daughter's cheek won't change anything, but there's nothing else she can do. The force of her slap knocks Tiana off her lap onto the dock. She's horrified by what she's done and she wants to hit her again, and then Layla's there.

"Shhh," Layla says. She puts her arms around Amanda and Amanda realizes that Layla's crying. Her own face is dry. "Shhh," Layla says again as she reaches to gather Tiana into her embrace. "Your momma didn't mean to hit you." Maybe Layla even believes that, but Amanda knows what she's done and knows exactly how much she meant it. When Layla explores the welt on Tiana's face with careful fingers, Amanda's as aware of the texture of her daughter's skin, the heat of bruised flesh, as if it were her own fingers.

"It's going to be okay," Layla says, but she's crying hard enough to hiccup. "We'll all get to the other side of the wall. Soon."

Amanda's anger is like lemon juice on metal, corrosive and sharp. She pulls away from Layla. The chocolate bar in her pocket bumps her upper thigh.

"Look what I've got for you," she says. She holds the chocolate up in front of Tiana's face. Tiana's eyelids have swollen from the tears she's holding back. She's sucking her thumb, wet hair plastered to her neck.

"You love chocolate," Amanda coaxes, hating herself. After a moment Tiana reaches for the chocolate. Amanda wants to tell her not to take it, but she drops the chocolate into Tiana's hand.

The dock bobs up and down with a rhythm like a heartbeat. Where the shadow of the wall ends, the water sparkles like an ad for a Caribbean vacation. When they first arrived at the camp, a strip of yellowing grass edged the sidewalk between the buildings. After the water rose, refracted sunlight transformed the grass into glowing gold beneath the water. The saltwater killed the grass within a few days, but first it made the dying grass beautiful.

That night after Layla has fallen asleep and Tiana has been still for so long on their shared cot that Amanda believes she's the only one in the room still awake, Tiana turns and burrows her face into Amanda's neck. "I saved you some," Tiana whispers.

Foil rustles and then Tiana presses a square of chocolate into Amanda's hand. Sorrow wells up in her as vast and inescapable as the water that's swallowing their refugee camp. "You have it, sweetie. The chocolate's for you." She finds Tiana's hand in the darkness and wraps her fingers around the chocolate.

"I didn't mean to make you mad," Tiana says. "I only wanted to see what the world looked like under the water."

"Under the water everything's more beautiful," Amanda whispers. "Right beneath us in the hall where you used to run, glittering blue mackerel swarm. The water foams white with the flicker of their tails. If you touched one, its scales would feel like velvet."

Tiana sighs and snuggles closer. The building rocks with the lullaby of the ocean.

"Pink and purple anemones lodge in the crevices of abandoned furniture." Amanda lays her cheek against Tiana's hair and inhales the smell of brine clinging to the curls. "Hermit crabs with legs the color of rubies scuttle across the bathroom tiles. A spiny pufferfish peeks out of the cupboard where you played hide and seek. Silver air bubbles cling to its spikes like beads on a wedding dress."

It's a bedtime story without a happy ending. "Do you still have that chocolate?" Amanda asks. She opens her mouth and lets Tiana feed her the square of chocolate. It melts on her tongue, chalky and bitter beneath the sweetness. She can't make herself swallow. The chocolate pools in the back of her mouth. The wall is only a darker part of the night outside her window.

Tiana's breath is even, her body heavy and relaxed. Finally Amanda does the thing that she's known she will have to do since the moment she opened her mouth and allowed Tiana to place the chocolate on her tongue. When she can no longer bear the feel of it in her mouth, when the bitterness has overwhelmed any residual sweetness, she swallows, because there is no other possible choice.

E. M. Wright's work has appeared or is forthcoming in *Berkeley Fiction Review*, *The South Carolina Review*, *Pithead Chapel*, and elsewhere. She holds an MFA from Vermont College of Fine Arts.

Dark Waters

Deborah L. Davitt

They never tell you how brown flood water is,
like thin gravy overflowing a plate;

that it's cold, that it smells like mildew—
or how heavy it is,
as you struggle to push
the car door open against the press of it,
the angry river like a giant
leaning against the car's side,
that if you do,
the water will sweep in, curling cold
against your legs in seconds.

They never mention that modern cars
don't have window-cranks anymore,
that they can't be opened without
the aid of the drowned engine—

they never suggest
that the highway system's designed
to channel water
like a mass of tangled rivers—
that we're living
in a delta that can't be seen
only inferred
through change over time,

or that the swamps
and the hungry ocean
are just waiting to take it all back.

Deborah L. Davitt was raised in Nevada, but currently lives in the flood-prone city of Houston, Texas with her husband and son, and has watched Hurricanes Ike and Harvey, as well as other, nameless storms, leave their marks since she moved there. Her poetry has received Rhysling, Dwarf Star, and Pushcart nominations; her short fiction has appeared in *Galaxy's Edge*, *Intergalactic Medicine Show*, and *Pseudopod*. For more about her work, including her Edda-Earth novels and her poetry collection, The Gates of Never, please see www.edda-earth.com.

Xoxoxoxoxo

Nicole Walker

I'm bad at leaving. My friends Monica and Jeff hosted a high school graduation party for their daughter Juliana on the back patio of an Oakmont restaurant. They served barbecued chicken and steak kabobs and deep-fried chicken rolls. I drank an eight-ounce glass of wine, which contributed to my not leaving. I told Erik I'd be home by 7, but at 7:30 I texted him to say I was on my way home. It took another half an hour to say goodbye to Leilah and Eric and Annette. I said goodbye to Monica and Jeff twice. I promised Tia we'd make real fried chicken this summer. I hugged Gioia Woods and asked her one more time about how happy her daughter was at Flagstaff High School. I'm spending half my time fretting over where my kids go to school. School choice, like leaving a party, is a miserable thing and takes too long. Rip it off like a Band-Aid. Pick a school. Go home. Leave before kissing Juliana congratulations one more time.

So I do leave, but I bring Karen home with me because if she's still with me, then the party is not over, even though I really do need to go to bed so I can wake up and pack for Iceland where I get to see you and we can talk about Y and Z.

But then at my house, there's more wine and more talk about school choice, and Erik comes to hang out even though he swore he was just going to stay in the other room and fall asleep on the couch because he doesn't have the same relationship to party and people that I have. But really, he does like people and parties and so he has a beer and Karen stays and we have one too many glasses of wine, but that's okay because it's still a little chilly at night and the door is wide open and even though Max is asleep on the futon at the foot of our bed, Erik and I wrap our legs around each other all night so I don't sleep that well, but I get up anyway and make the kids' lunches and take the dogs for a run and get to work grading and editing and writing about saying goodbye, which I really hate to do.

Every day I don't die is a good one. It makes me grateful, the prospect of death. Today the plants we call red hot pokers poked their red heads up like matchsticks, friction against sky blue air, and the blue flax, more moisture than friction, lives, and the kitten that got thrown out of a window lives. The kid with the cough lives and the kid who got lost in the forest lives.

Yesterday wasn't as good a day. The kids immigrating from Libya drowned, and the girl who survived the Manchester bombings succumbed to her injuries, and Denis Johnson died, and although I didn't love him as much as everyone else seems to on the Facebook, I still hate to say goodbye.

You and I will meet in Iceland where we will not have to say goodbye. The sun won't set. We'll stay up all night remembering how we began this project, on a different, warmer beach. We will sit and stare out at the old harbor and think that maybe one of these molecules of water has traveled all the way from the Southern Ocean (are we still calling it that?) to say not goodbye but hello to us. There will be no polar bears there to die, nor any reindeer, and even the puffin is extant enough to appear on the touristy menus.

Maybe if we never go home and maybe if the sun never sets and maybe if we figure out how to linger without drinking too much wine, we won't have to say goodbye. We won't have to come to a conclusion. We won't have to sign off. The humpback whales. I can see it in the distance. They're coming back. Maybe all intelligent life doesn't destroy itself. Maybe it just bides its time.

Nicole Walker is the author of the collections *The After-Normal: Brief, Alphabetical Essays on a Changing Planet* from Rose Metal Press and *Sustainability: A Love Story* from Mad Creek Books. Her previous nonfiction work includes *Where the Tiny Things Are*, *Egg*, *Micrograms*, *Quench Your Thirst with Salt*, and a book of poems, *This Noisy Egg*. She wishes she'd gone with the original title for her collection of poems, "Comeuppance," so she only had one book with "Egg" in the title, but like eggs or chickens, the poetry collection came first.

"Xoxoxoxoxo" originally appeared in *The After-Normal* in 2019.

Happenstance

Fran Wilde

Sunlight hits the top floor of One Eastwaters Tower in a hard, bright wave. When the afternoon glow also strikes the lake, everything turns to dazzle.

I've lived high-lakeside for three years. I still startle at the ripple of water-light on the floor, dappling my skin, sparking off the bits of my exoskel that are otherwise invisible no matter what I'm wearing.

People are hardwired for pattern and expectation. Changes shock the system.

I think about this a lot. Especially when I'm working.

Shake off the dazzle, Lane. Focus on Eastwaters' maps, the Happenstance Engineering Overlay. A fingertip pinch here, a pull there, and you're done. Got to hit quota before end of day and it's already late afternoon.

Patterns mean safety. Known risks instead of unknown hazards. A smooth experience.

See also: boredom and stagnation.

So the city gave a handful of Happenstance Engineers full access to the roadworks, the waterworks. With a fast calculation on the city-physics engine and some caution signs, I start an alleyway shift near Water Street. Over a few days' time, the quiet Eastwaters alley will begin to run east-west for a block. That moves several small shops onto the main thoroughfare, out from the shadows. And it means Sam Bergo from Tower Two, seventeenth floor, and Juliette Dory, Tower Seven, floor twenty, will meet by accident on the way to work the day before their first CrossTowers date.

That's a couple quota boxes checked with a single job.

On the Overlay, I let the meter run out two minutes early on a single seat at El Fortuna's open four-top. A Solar Toys CEO is using two more seats as a remote office. Now I watch the dataflow as Zai Norcelli "accidentally" takes a seat. Before the new CEO of SolarToys realizes Zai isn't the person they're meeting for dinner, Zai has awkwardly answered questions about his custom automatons and passed a business card.

Check two.

Earbud pings break my concentration: once, twice. An inner-circle chat. That could only mean Sirocco.

"Sorry, working," I whisper.

Siro's probably staring at his palm in consternation at that. If he really wants me, he knows where to find me.

Ha. The thought makes me smile.

I toy with the idea of making a fountain rise from the intersection at King and Vorhees, way up on Eastwaters's last hill within megacity limits, settle for a less-whimsical pothole instead. Less likely to get me in trouble with the city, or the water division of Civil Engineering. Foot traffic will still have to go around the obstacle and people will still shift their day slightly. Bonus: I'm all the way at the edge of my territory. That's three.

So much for patterns, city dwellers. The changes I've made to the smart streets and shops start to ripple in real time: people bump into each other to avoid the pothole, grumble a lot, and commiserate. On their new path, they discover that small, out of the way shop with that thing they didn't know they needed. The shop will drop City Engineering a thank you cred, and some of that will slide to me. Check, check, check.

I can almost hear Eastwaters's gears click into new shapes; the streets sing. But city infrastructure isn't my watch. Gears, physics, street sounds, and lights belong to CivE and MechE. Those engineers listen for the grind and crunch, the rush of water, the sound of a tram barreling along a tunnel.

My skel—an old model, but I keep it because I've made my own mods—chimes quietly. New message from Siro.

"Text and scroll." The command sends his words to my wraparounds—the only part of the skel I can take off because they're just for work. *:: Dinner 7pm w. VC VP Ok? @Home ::*

It's 5:15 pm now. The depth of my sigh sets the suit's monitors whirring, trying to figure out what's the matter with Lane. *Pain? Exhaustion?* "Stand down."

Annoyance isn't on the suit's checklist.

:: Okay ::

I wave the message away. For a moment, the sun-sparkled hypercarbon of my skel transfixes me. The light snakes from my palms, up past my elbows, and on back past the edges of my tank top. The skel looks like stars.

I'm not going to soft-pedal Siro. He knows that two hours is nowhere near enough time for me to get ready and be entertaining. He can handle the party himself.

Sure enough he texts right back. *:: Catering at 6:45 ::*

The skel stops trying to assess me as soon as my blood pressure drops back into normal range. Need to jack those metrics down a bit. Siro likes to know how I'm feeling, but I don't, not this much. This is way too sensitive.

On my wraparounds, the city maps illuminate new connections built off the Happenstances I've put down. My earjacks feed me snippets of laughter. That's a day's pay when you're a Hap Engineer. The sound of cred micropayments from the city grant going into my account. The kick of unexpected meetings and faces lighting up.

Most cities, even a few years ago? My activities might have been called mayhem. But in a smart city where everything runs on smooth, automated rails? Happy accidents have to be engineered.

I bag my Haps quota when a banana shortage I caused at Tower One's grocery pays off. To celebrate, I vent the overhead water feed on Tower Seventeen's second floor vertical farm. Just a little.

Points of reference light up all over the megatowers as people come out to see the rainbows. The points grow brighter still as the fish in the atrium breeding ponds rise to nibble on the fruit dropped by the soaked plants. Beautiful. More lights intersect as neighbors reconnect beneath the rain and sunbows. That district's social nodes go bright purple on the map.

Check.

5:50 p.m. I need to move the printing supplies off the dining room table and get changed. But I want to watch Davian Mirren's payoff once it filters down the network. Mirren needed bananas for the desert she'd looked up at work that morning. Right after I'd shorted the grocery, my mark had to find a different store. She chose the next tower over, used the crosswalk, grumbled at the inefficiency. On the way there, she met an old friend from college on her regular run. My cred record showed Davian applying for a new job at her friend's company. Excellent.

My weekly Haps quota—upper left in my wraparounds and

lower right on the main map projected above my loft's coffee table—both go green. It's only Wednesday, and though I'm still short on the month because I took sick leave last week, I'm catching up.

I stretch my hands and pull the wraparounds from my eyes. Drop them on the coffee table. Resist the urge to sink into the couch and watch the sun on the lake. My loft's a big open square on the forty-sixth floor. When I found it, the tower hadn't been popular; all the city's hotspots were up the hill near all the good restaurants and clubs. Tower One had been a loss leader for a failed developer who didn't understand Eastwaters's docks, so I locked in cheap rent and camped out, eating takeout on the sofa—my main furniture besides the matterprinter and a mattress—watching sunsets through the big windows, avoiding the Oldtown protests, and working.

The plexi coffee table came in a few weeks ago, along with the chrome dining set, the retro lamps, and Siro.

"You timed the market, Lane," he'd said. "This neighborhood's getting hot." His sheepish grin did the asking for him and, tired of pushing myself to get across town for dates, I let him move in.

Don't date your boss. I know, I know.

I could say he was closest to hand. We worked together for years. But truth was, I liked him. And he was never shocked by my mods. When I told him. He didn't mind the skel, and he wasn't creepy about it. That was important.

Plus, his codework was damn sexy. Even his comments.

OK, I admit our code those first few years got pretty not safe for work, but it was just us, working on the Happenstance algorithm. Things just . . . happened.

And now I'm cleaning up so he can have investors over for dinner.

My skel chimes. "Stand down. Recalibrate for less input." The skel chimes again, acknowledging.

I box the printing supplies—plastic and chrome for modding the skel, a few carbon tubes for reinforcements—and shove that under the sofa with my foot. The printer itself Siro will have to move. It's too heavy for me, even with the exoskeleton's help. Some skels are work-strong, but this one is mostly support, a little reinforcement to keep my limbs from popping, a little skin-level pain-soothe. The basics.

I grab a short, sheer black dress from the bedroom closet and wiggle it over my head. Leave my jeans on. Siro wants fancier? He can damn well let me know before noon. Swap my chucks for flats. Don't bother about the hair, which drops straight down my back like a second brace, no matter what I do to it. Check.

I have a few minutes more to watch the map before I have to deal with guests. The map soothes me. I can't always watch the ripples caused by Happenstances, but the metrics drop from the network to the Happenstance Engineering Overlay in a few hours. Even without metrics, I can see I'm having a good day, just by the glow of the overlay. New nodes in the network are strengthening. I know it's good work.

The algorithms Siro and I developed over the past three years and the lines we'd patched through the city's main utility systems—plus social, shopping, traffic, and scheduling apps—were light-fast responsive. That made the work easier. Not just for me. For the two other Happenstance Engineers we'd partnered with in Eastwaters also, and for the Haps in Seattle and Shenzhen who were pioneering the system there.

A knock on the door. I wave it open from the middle of the loft and go back to work. Siro's caterers can set up the table however they want.

Smells like salmon. Big meeting then, if Siro's springing for real fish.

I haven't played big with the map shifts today—I'd burned a few of those from my quota last week. Today is smalls—the most fun, in my opinion. They cause the most direct Happenstances. I like the up close shifts, the changes in just a few lives that one pause or a new conversation create.

The Happenstance overlay on the map glows brighter in that edge district. The one with the pothole. Shit, maybe that was too much. That's a lot more people than usual in that district.

My skel pings softly again—suit charge alert this time. I ignore it for now. Still enough power in the system to support my legs and back. The map's got my attention.

With a double click, the thick door to the loft opens, then slams closed. I barely hear it.

A few moments later, Siro's fingers brush the bare edge of my ear. "You are an artist," he says.

He always says that.

"I like the connections." Leaning into the touch, I douse my maps.

Lakelight plays on Siro's chrome gearbag, dropped on the coffee table. Dazzling. The sleeve of his grey suit's dappled in light.

"Besides, you built the damn nodes. I just play them." I turn to look at him. When he smiles shyly, I add, "Quit that. You *know* it's elegant."

He's a weaver of networks. A maker of gates. All I do is help people walk through.

"You play a great tune." Siro slides an arm around my waist, hard exoskeleton and all. Smells like cologne, bright wood tones, but not too much—so he'd been meeting with the city again—plus garlic and thai basil—he'd had lunch at his favorite pho place.

My stomach growls. "A lunch meeting and a dinner?"

"Have to, Lane. Eastwaters isn't going to run Happenstance off grants much longer. Utilities won't let us in unless we hand over the algorithm, and then we can't expand to more cities. I'd rather go private. Contract to the city."

We'd talked about this before. I liked my job better than his. "Who's in the net tonight?"

Before we'd proved the Happenstance concept in Tower Sixteen—on the upper edge of the city, where Siro lived—no one would sit down with him. First sign of our success had been "Caledin," a competitive food-dance gig that had grown out of an accidental cross-scheduling of two community groups. Yeah, it was as messy as it sounds.

No one realized Caledin was going to be big until it caught on in three more towers, both players and watchers. Soon after, a support group appeared for school children who couldn't use VR gear—something the city government hadn't even known was a problem until two disparate parents met in a fifth floor grocery over the last bag of oranges.

It wasn't long before metrics supported so much of a shift for the better in Tower Sixteen—more students coming to classes, more residents attending events—that the tower and several more around it began to pay us. Give us access to more systems.

Sure, there were a few disasters that first outing—a flooded apartment, people who were so late to work they got docked—and we took the cred hit for that. But we learned a lot too. Three years on, people across the towers are happier, more connected. They don't get stuck in ruts as much. The data shows it. Hell, the maps show it.

Except for the map that was lighting up too much before I had to stow it. Shit, why now?

Siro hasn't answered me about who's coming to dinner either. I repeat the question.

He smiles his best please-don't-hate-me grin. "Octavian Smith."

"I don't need to be here for this."

Octavian's the worst kind of player. He likes to fund companies with pretty owners or pretty assets. He seeded the first part of the Happenstance trial run, actually told people he'd invented it, and then ditched for a higher profile project. We'd nearly lost everything, Siro and me.

Now we were successful and Octavian was back. "How can you consider him?"

My partner's smile falters. "He's got the best offer, Lane."

With the suit sensitivity turned down, I can seethe and he'll never hear a thing. "It's the only offer, right?"

Instead of answering, Siro busies himself, taking the lids off the catering trays, pouring wine. Fish, rice, beans. The table's set for three and he's not changing that. My appetite goes dead.

I tap my left arm twice. The skel beeps obligingly. "I'm going outside to charge."

"Lane, now?" Siro says.

But I'm already out on the balcony watching the sunset. Not much in the way of charging at this point in the day, but the colors are pretty. A flock of birds skids in random patterns over the lake.

Back inside, Octavian and Siro are standing on the other side of the glass, watching me. God, that guy.

Where Siro's pale from head to toe—greying hair, light-steel eyes—Octavian's bright and right on trend. Man loves his lips. Right now, he's wearing two tones: chrome top, purple bottom. His polychrome jacket looks orange, then purple in the right light.

"Lane," he gushes when I come back in. "Such a pleasure. Your stats are amazing. And Siro's told me about your mods." He hands me a bouquet of stargazer lilies. The smell is overpowering.

My face heats up.

"She embarrasses easily," Siro chuckles. I could almost murder him and then print out his casket and drop it into the lake.

"It's not embarrassment," I say. "I'd rather my stats and mods stayed out of negotiations, is all."

Octavian's smile brightens. "I like a challenge."

Siro looks at me, pleadingly.

Octavian tries again. "This is such a fantastic apartment. Lane, you had such vision grabbing this one."

Better. "Thank you." But I don't smile. I'm not interested in anything Octavian's selling.

Over dinner, Octavian's smile just gets bigger as he and Siro talk. By the time I go to bed, they've started drawing up plans, talking acquisitions. Loudly.

Damn. I *like* my job. I don't want Octavian anywhere near it. Maybe not Siro either.

The next morning, while Siro sleeps off the wine, I watch more points on the Happenstance overlay begin to glow brighter, this time near the alley I'm shifting.

"Want to get dinner outside the tower tonight?" Siro collapses on the sofa, a glint in his eyes. "Surprises."

I'm in no mood. "Tell me now. I hate surprises." Especially Octavian surprises.

Siro gloats. "You do surprises for a living! How can you hate them?" But he squeezes my hand. "It's going to be great. New project, Lane."

Maybe it's not Octavian? I shrug. "Sure." I could like surprises, with enough advance warning. "I have to finish this quota set." I put my wraps on, but keep the main map off. I can't afford to fall any further behind, especially if Siro's seriously considering Octavian. Maybe I can work in Seattle. Once I solve this overload bug.

The system's set up so that Happenstance Engineers can synchronize across the city so that no one area gets more changes—and more serendipity—over another. Quotas and data keep everything balanced.

"It's good, I promise." Siro grins. "Hey, Octavian wasn't kidding about your cred . . . ."

I wave him off. "Later?" That small square of the map's glowing more brightly than last night. Too many people with too much Happenstance is bad. Kind of like too much of one kind of data overflowing one part of a system and leaving the rest blank.

Siro shrugs. "Of course. I'm going to get cleaned up anyway." He leaves the bag on the table and closes the bedroom door behind him.

Everyone in Eastwaters has cred based on work quotas, thank yous from friends, community goodwill. Micropayments sometimes add up, though I donate most of mine to biomech research a couple of cities over. But with Siro and Octavian both talking about my cred, I take a peek on my wraps. Okay, it's worth more than a little today. Something I'd done had gotten a big gratitude bump.

Grinning, I keep working. I can buy extra supplies for my printer with that. The map brightens again, same spot, right near the alley. Too many people there.

Might have to shut it down. That will ding me, but it's better than having something go wrong. Happenstance can get messy if you're not careful.

But shutting down the shift isn't as important as figuring out where the bug is in the algorithm. How did people know to go where everything is shifting? I'm always careful to cloak my actions, so no one expects.

I heat water for tea in the kitchen. The caterers have come and cleaned up. That's great because my hands are shaky. The skel struggles to brace my wrists and fingers, but this isn't my crappy joints. This is nerves.

A similar in-a-rut pattern emerged after one of my early engineering runs. I'd ignored it and that's how I'd besieged an entire floor with kittens. Long story. Longer cleanup. Don't ask.

Now I can't help worrying. This isn't like the kittens or the flooding. People are gravitating toward where I'm working. They're anticipating and—worse—hanging around, *waiting* for happenstance.

"That's not how it works, kids." I shut the alley shift down. "Sorry, Sam. Sorry, Juliette."

If my work is becoming part of a pattern that people can

anticipate somehow, that breaks the whole system.

My suit chimes again. I ignore it. Throw a frustrated poll onto the network instead. It doesn't look like anything much—small, reward-based, single question. *:: Do you think luck is hard to find? ::*

I'd seeded two other polls over the past three weeks. The results all came back the same. This one does too.

An increasing percentage of people say no. I watch as real time results creep past 45%.

So strange.

I get the Happenstance Engineers in Seattle and Shenzhen up on my screen, but hold off on grabbing the two in Eastwaters. They're aren't online yet anyway and, besides, they work for Octavian.

"Seeing anything strange in your nodes?"

The engineer in Shenzhen shakes his head. "Nothing unusual."

Seattle hangs onto the connection longer. "Check for scanners on the networks. We've had bots lately scanning keywords. We're shifting to codes and false phrases in order to gain a bit of a head start on them."

"Thanks. That could be the answer I need." I take off the wraps. Look up to find Siro on the sofa with the main map open, watching my moves.

"Hey." Too flustered to get really mad yet, I sit down next to him. Him opening my map is concerning. He's never done that before.

"Tell me." He knows something's up.

That's *genuinely* concerning, since I don't have a grip on the data yet. "There's nothing to tell."

Siro frowns by halves, one side of his mouth dropping to match the other. "Spill, Lane." Hung over, for sure.

I play with my wraps and then drop them on the table. Look out at the balcony, the lake beyond. The dazzle's just about to break, but the sun's not low enough yet.

"That thing I was talking about with Seattle?" I assume he heard. "I think people are starting to expect luck. All the time. That ruins the algorithm. Happenstance? Serendipity? Can't be expected. None of our quotas will mean anything if all we're doing is filling a hole that keeps getting bigger because of expectations. We won't help anyone connect, we'll just make another rut."

I think of the family yesterday who'd just "lucked into" a long lost relative by the farm levels after the mini-flood in Tower Seventeen. Of the happy reunion photos that had spread across the network. I love helping nudge that sort of thing along. I don't want to give it up because the algorithm's obsolete.

Must be a way to fix it. Code words like Seattle? Just a kludge. I want a real mod. Something that evolves.

Siro has gone wraps-up, messaging someone. He'll be little help until he's over his hangover anyway.

On the balcony outside my flat, a seagull lands, then tucks its wings and cocks its head as it ponders the broad glass doors. I slide the doors open and step outside, "Shoo!"

My suit chimes as sunlight hits it, charging back up.

So that's the jittery wrists. Note for a future mod: something to help me tell the difference between nerves and tech failure. Like, say, any number of chimes from my exoskeleton. I make another note.

I'd forgotten I needed to get to full charge. Possibly for a couple days. The skel drains easier on lower charge, and one of my new mods might be dragging the system. Either way, I hadn't remembered to charge until I saw the bird.

People forget to help themselves sometimes when they're busy, when everything's in easy reach.

Below the balcony, the city spreads out on all sides in a neat grid. The lake fans against the horizon also, but with less pattern, more sunlight sparkling across the water.

Siro slides the doors open, snakes a finger down the back of my neck. "Sorry. Rough night." Hands me a glass. Ice water. The ice is luxurious. He sips a gin tonic.

"I don't know why you want to deal with Octavian again," I say. Never really good at knowing when to cut my losses, me. "This mess worries me."

"We'll figure it out," Siro says. "You always come up with interesting approaches. Dinner's canceled though. Octavian says we've got to clean up Happenstance before we can court more buyers. He's got some structural ideas—new nodes, line of sight stuff."

Not just Octavian, then. A group of them, eventually. Another of Octavian's schemes. Suddenly I feel very tired. "When were you going to tell me?"

"Tell you what?"

That you were selling me out. "A group of buyers?" Things are going to change. Damn I love this job. More than anything. It lets me be in the world if I want, when I want. It lets me make a difference.

I lean my head back, hold out my arms so the sun can hit more of the skel. The servos whir softly as the braces shift to support my back and keep my knees from dislocating. Joints. Intersections. Big old fail points. Especially if your system's not making enough of what holds them together.

"You'll figure it out," Siro repeats. He's donned his wraps again, reading. "I can get some node programmers to help you if you want." His voice has that tin quality of someone half paying attention. He's like this a lot lately, not wanting to sort out details with just me, assuring everyone everything will be fine.

"But don't mention it to anyone, not yet. Not until something changes." He looks at me over the wraps until I nod.

I stare out over the lake, looking for something to change out there. For a fish to jump, a waterspout, anything. "You told Octavian." What I don't say yet: Aside from shutting down the program, like I shut down the alley shift, I can't see a way out of the rut. Worse, with Siro in the loft, I know I can't work on the problem all night the way I want to: letting the wraps wear a red mark on the bridge of my nose, letting my suit run out of charge from lack of sunlight. No, because dinners and Siro dragging me outside or telling me to "spill" before I'm ready.

Check: still mad.

But Siro's gone back inside. Didn't hear me. Time to tell him to take a walk for a bit.

67% charge on the skel. Good enough. I pull the doors open.

In the loft's greatroom, Siro has an expensive loafer up on the coffee table. He points at the map. "Hey, here's another ten percent on the node." He shakes his head. "Just waiting. Like they think it's going to rain candy or something. They've been doing this for a while?"

"Yeah."

"Don't worry. We'll fix everything. Octavian's got an idea. He's coming over."

That doesn't sound like a fix at all. "You creeped my live feed again?"

Siro really needs to take a walk.

It's still my loft. I haven't added his name to the lease yet. Granted, it's a handshake lease, not all that legal, done when everyone wanted to live up the hill. Doesn't really matter if he's on it or not.

In the quiet, I can hear my skel ticking. I can hear Siro's breathing. It's smooth and relaxed, like he's keeping himself calm. I modded a data feed upgrade last week—that's probably what was sucking the skel's power dry. That was why the sick leave. But now I'm glad I did. The added room sensors and proximity monitors in the skel let me watch Siro's heartbeat and blood pressure. Even when I brush my leg against his thigh, he's dead steady.

Lying. Siro. And so careful about it. "I just wanted to see for myself. There's an easy fix, you know."

Fine. I can lie too, and he doesn't have the upgrades to sense it. My hand twitches. The recharged skel balances to compensate. "Go on."

"Octavian's solution? He's thinking we upgrade some of the land nodes. One node to start, to see if it makes a difference in predictability. Somewhere unusual, like Oldtown."

Yeah, well, Octavian owns a big share of a node company. And shares in the other two Hap groups. We just own the algorithm.

Siro catches a faceful of my opinion. "Shit, Lane, he's just got an idea. Hear him out, okay? We can't do this fast without you anyway."

There's one aspect to installing new nodes that I can do easily. I'm a walking data center—even more than Siro knows. When I move through the city, my skel can pick up data from my surroundings, anything that isn't marked private or no-entry. My maps load to my suit as easily as they do to the loft's coffee table. I can engineer Happenstances from anywhere and see the results at ground level. I just prefer to be up high. Out of the noise. Away from the people. The other Haps can't do that. Not without huge rigs and a fair bit of claustrophobia from not being used to the gear.

I'm very used to the gear.

"Sure." I'm tired. Siro knows it. And the minute I say sure, he drops the guilt-face and blinks at his wraps. They go opaque like someone's been waiting on the other side of the connection. The data sleeve Siro wears lights up. Three swipes and a quick reply cascade bracelets his arm. His wraps go transparent again. "Great. Octavian's coming now."

That's fast. "Didn't Octavian just leave a couple hours ago? He must have slept in an empty flat in the tower. Can't we go somewhere else? This is still my place."

Siro pulls me close. "We live here now, remember? Not just you." He runs a thumb along my throat where the skel doesn't need to support me. My skin goosebumps in the worst way. I lean away from it, feeling the warmth Siro's hand leaves across my throat. I don't want that right now. Too much.

I'd let him in, sure. Let him stay. But this place is still mine. He'd wanted it that way, especially at first. For years, he'd kept his things and his meetings at Tower Seventeen. Didn't want to complicate things. I found this apartment. Created my nest. Never thought it would become one of the most sought-after towers in the city.

I just liked the height, the view. Now he likes it too.

When Octavian knocks on the door, I let Siro get it. I'd already seen Octavian coming down the hall on my wraps—yep, I modded the hallway too. I know he's carrying more stargazers, even though I dumped last night's stargazers in the garbage as soon as I could.

It's going to be one of those meetings.

Siro lets Octavian into the loft. "Thanks for coming back."

Octavian holds out the flowers so I have to take them, be responsible for them, while he and Siro begin talking. I leave them high and dry by the sink.

"So," Octavian's saying. They have my map projected over the coffee table. Again without asking. "Lane, you're the best Happenstance person we've got. You make it look so effortless. With a few adjustments, we should be up and running with no expectation factor in a few days. Easy."

Really. I haven't been able to figure out how. I wonder at this. My shoulders tighten the more I think about it. Nothing's that easy.

And who gave Octavian the right to say "we?" I haven't accepted yet. My skel tries to get me to relax, applying modulated pressure to muscles in my back. Screw that. I shrug it off. I want to be angry.

Octavian fills in the space left by my silence. "People don't value the work that goes into Happenstance. Just like folks used to leave the faucets running before they installed the timeout meters."

Siro nods in complete agreement.

"Sometimes you just want to take a long shower." I'm growling now.

Siro sighs and opens the doors to the balcony. No birds out there now. No dazzle either. Just the real city's grid expanding out from the lakefront below.

Octavian points, down and to the left. To Oldtown. "To plant the node, we need you to go to Oldtown, by the phở shop, and open up a new line."

"A line too? In Oldtown?" Lines, like everything else in the smart cities, have to be cleared with the city. A direct line-of-sight control on all the hypercarbon embeds in city structure? So much paperwork. Siro was all about the clearances so I didn't press. If he was signing off, this was legit.

That was Siro's favorite takeout place anyway.

"Just a temp line." Octavian nods. "It'll be like old times before we'd laid down any of the Happenstance nodes."

We. Again. I don't recall Octavian running any lines three years ago. Just dropping some cash and running away.

"A temp line to do what? There aren't any smart streets or pop-up builds for blocks beyond Tower Seven in Oldtown."

"There are a couple nearby. You dropped a pocket park just across the street from where we're going, so it's line-of-sight to the next node. The couple there run a grocery and the phở shop, in a three-story tucked into Tower Seven's shadow, east side. They'll let you up on the roof for sight access," Octavian answers. But it isn't an answer, not really.

The sun hits the lake, white diamonds sparkle on the tower glass.

Three-story walk-ups are rare now, except in Oldtown. But the skel makes stairs easier.

Siro clears his throat. "You'll just need to grab their data key in order to loop them in. I'll do the rest."

"What's the rest?" *And who grabs anyone's data key anymore?*

"Bigger Happenstance. A new way to push things forward. The walk-up is at a great location for line of sight access to five towers. So there can be more randomness, and people might not be able to predictive-jump the Happenstance spots so frequently. Also bigger. Did I mention?"

I hesitate.

Octavian looks at Siro with a meaningful eyebrow raised, then sits down on the sofa and pats it, trying to get me to come sit too. "Come on, Lane. Show me the mods you've been doing. Compared to them, a node install is a cakewalk."

I don't move. There's a long silence.

"She's an engineer, not a prop," Siro finally says. "You don't get to play with her."

"I can speak for myself." Annoyance doesn't register on the skel, thank everything. I pick the bench just beyond Octavian's reach. Ignore his interest in my mods. "What do you bring to this?" And what has Siro promised you?

"The new algorithm gives you enough variation that your activities will be invisible to your districts. You'll be invisible to almost anyone until you're right on top of them. Better than that, it will give you some surprises too."

"I don't want surprises. I don't want your code. Siro's code is fine."

Octavian purses his lips and clenches his thick fingers in his lap. "That's unfortunate. My review of your work says you could use some surprises."

The leather-analog surface of the bench I'm sitting on is cool to the touch. While my skel whirs, adjusting support, I trace the bench's upholstery: circles, triangles. The minute stitching, the three-ply thread, and the woven padding beneath.

His review of my work. "I don't see why."

Siro clears his throat. "Lane, doing a deal with the cities meant we had to look hard at everything. That turned up some questions about whether your work has been giving you unfair advantages. Whether you had some bias in your project selection. Octavian offered to look into it when we hired him to solve the predictability problem a couple of weeks ago."

They'd brought Octavian on around when I'd first noticed

the problem. Before I'd said anything. Siro had known for that long and not said a word.

Couple weeks since he'd moved in, too. I felt physically ill.

"I couldn't say anything because the city had questions. And I didn't want to upset you. Make you sick." He tilts his head. "Okay?"

I mute my skel's alerts. Not okay.

I'd taken nothing for myself. Worked ridiculous hours for nothing. Met all my quotas once we landed the grant.

"I get to decide, remember?" I decide what I can and cannot handle. "How have I been unfair? My data's clean."

Octavian jumps in. "Your data's wrong."

Siro puts out a steadying hand. "Just subconscious bias; it can be fixed."

Then Octavian's saying, "You've been missing things for a while. Given your condition . . . ." That makes me want to toss them both into the sun.

Then don't let them say that to you. Push back.

"My condition's got nothing to do with my work. And my data's good."

"I wish that was the case," Octavian says. His voice turns velvet. He's so very sorry. "But my assessment doesn't lie."

"It does. This time it does. Whatever you have, it's nothing I've done."

Velvet-voiced and oh so sorry, Octavian spreads out data sheets on the table.

"Here's a list of your last hundred Happenstances. They're all well distributed. You've been working very consciously to make sure everyone gets a fair chance. But . . . ." He flipped another data sheet. "Here's the value on your flat. And your cred." The numbers climb. I can see the pattern, almost—but . . . it looks strange. With every happenstance, my value, and the value of the one thing that's mine, rises, based on Octavian's calculations.

"You think I'm enriching myself? Making this neighborhood more popular?"

"Not consciously, no." Octavian plays with a twitch-ring, moving the gears back and forth. "Just by being you? Maybe. The city's concerned. You're in a very important position, especially if we become contractors. We want to make sure everything is . . . clear." We again. I realize he's offering me something. I don't want it.

Siro continues, "So we're here to help you optimize and modify. The first step is setting this node, giving yourself some unpredictability in your districts. If you're willing to do that, the city can see the rest is an accident."

"A little diversification of your investments won't hurt either," Octavian adds.

A deep breath feels like fire in my nostrils. "Diversification of what?"

"Yes. Your cred, your investments. You need to look cleaner for the city to take us as a consultant. Your loft too. It's rocketed in value. If you sublet it, or move, you won't look quite so complicit."

I shake my head. "I have too much work to do to deal with this bullshit. You two should take your data somewhere else." No way am I moving when I don't want to.

Sensing the resistance, Octavian puts a hand on Siro's shoulder. "Maybe we should do this later, over dinner."

"Do what?" I say. I run through the other things I've bought—three pairs of shoes, a few tunics to go over the skel. Some music.

Octavian's rich clothes and expensive hair are just the start of his investments, I know.

Siro, too. He looks carved, toned. He's been cleaning up a lot better lately. And me?

"How long have you been collecting data on me?"

Octavian shrugs. "Not on you, Lane. Never. Just on your work for us."

For at least as long as Siro's been in the apartment, then. My skin crawls beneath the frame of my skel.

Siro reaches out to me across the space between sofa and bench. I stare at his hand, hoping it bursts.

"I was concerned. Worried for you. Then Octavian said . . ."

"I know what Octavian's saying," I interrupt. "What do you want me to do to fix it?" When they say I can't do something, that makes me want to do it twice.

Octavian smiles at Siro. "I told you she'd want to help." He moves to the bench, sits beside me, and takes one of my hands. I can retract the braces, but I don't. He gets a fistful of hypercarbon and chrome. It feels rude.

I'm okay with rude.

Siro ignores the gesture. Sits on my other side, puts his arm around me. "You just need to run that one line. Drop one node. Everyone will see how much you want to help, and it will be fixed. Fast, too. The system will be so much more robust."

"They might not want that much luck. Not in Oldtown." Sandwiched between the two of them, I feel like a three-story walk-up shadowed by megatowers. "People don't like too much change. Just enough that it's a discovery."

Siro withdraws his arm. "You said you'd go." He needs me to go. *Why?*

"And I will. I'll go now." It's not yet late afternoon. I grab the chrome gearbag. Leave Siro and Octavian sitting around the coffee table.

As soon as the loft door shuts, I un-mute my skel. Every notice goes off. Pulse, breathing, tension, pain.

"Stand down." The skel quiets.

Going will fix the problem.

So. I'll go.

Where the upper lofts in Eastwaters are filled with light, the lifts are narrow and dark. Odd feeling, being encased thrice, once by my skel, once by the lift, then by the tower itself.

People crowd me too.

Descending the lift in Tower One, I'm trapped in a full-surround argument. Yelling, waving hands. Pushing.

Not my argument. Drunk couple. From a floor below, who'd been up to the roof.

"You don't understand," the pushing one says loudly. "I forgot I was supposed to meet you. It disappeared from my calendar."

They'd met over a calendar snafu, I knew.

Waving-hands just groans. "You forget about me all the time." The doors open and the couple steps out onto the market and gym floor of Tower Three in a dark silence.

I ride the rest of the way to street level alone. On the wall near the lift controls, someone's posted a note, using a pen and actual paper. "I've not been outside in ages. If you have a dog you want walked, or want company walking one, flag me on the network?"

The tear-offs where people take contact info off the sign are all gone.

People hunger to connect and don't know how any more.

I flex my fingers and my skel flexes with me. I know how. But can I keep helping without gaining unfair advantage?

I'd no intention of enriching myself, even subconsciously. Just thinking of it horrifies me. That Octavian has data on it? That's even worse.

My skel beeps. "Stand down." I know my heart rate's still way off. I can feel it in my temples. The skel pings again, ignoring me. Lights up a display on my wrist: orange bars—Power down to 45%. Not red yet, but I sure could have used some more charging time before I left. Shit.

But I'd been too angry to stay.

Make the node Octavian wants and get them both out of my hair. Then I can think.

What will I do if I can't Happenstance?

Another ping, this time from the Haps overlay. Fail report. My pothole has caused three bikers to collide. My cred takes a ding, then keeps falling as more people come out to see what the fuss is. I watch it drop. I pull my wraps up, leave them half-opaque in case someone else gets on the lift. I want to be able to see. Open up the map to have a look.

The accident's near the pothole all right. I adjust so that it will be less dangerous. Slide a garbage can on seamless magnetic controls across the street with a swipe. Redirect people even more around the approach to the area.

With the wraps on, I can't miss the notice from my building manager as it flickers its way into my inbox. Let it go until later. I have a mess to clean up.

Two more nudges and my cred stabilizes. But I've undone two big haps from yesterday. My quotas are in the hole now too. A complete mess. No one to blame but myself.

The lift stops, the doors slide open. Right into the lobby. Empty.

Outside, I stop, caught between the sunlit lake and the towers. Feel the exposed lines of my skel warm and begin to charge. Better.

Then I swing left onto a street between Tower Three and Tower Six. Head for Oldtown, and the takeout place.

The high towers immediately block lake and sunlight. The dappled shadows of reflected windows aren't enough to charge a piece of paper, much less smart carbon.

By the time I reach the shop, my skel's at 30%.

Powersuck. Shadows. And the phở place is caught up in Tower Seven's shadow. I'll have to work fast to place the node or I'll be crawling back to my loft. No thanks.

"Come on," I tell my legs. First thought: *Faster.* But no. That will suck power too. I'm really not the most efficient body out here. But the suit has two hours of charge left if I'm careful. I set it on low-power. Noisy but it'll get me through.

Octavian's new line and node will take an hour, tops.

Finally, I spot the front of the walk-up, with the smart towers built up and over it. Happens a lot in Oldtown, where brickwork and six-over-six windows are slowly devoured by the smartbuildings.

One of Just Phở's owners stands outside, arms folded. She watches me cross. Hears the low-power whine of my joints. "What's that?" She glances at her building, as if looking for cracks.

"Me," I try. "I'm a Happenstance engineer. They told you I was coming, they said?"

The owner nods. She doesn't smile.

In the shade where we're standing, I don't think she can see my skel.

"Won't take a second. I did a little work just up the smart side of the street." I point at the small pocket park I'd dropped. Where there'd once been a blank intersection, now there was a jungle gym and a colorful merry-go-round. Two kids playing, parents standing quietly nearby.

"That was nice work," she finally says.

My wraps say the owner's name is Pham Thi Bao Lan.

Mrs. Pham frowns. "What kind of install are you doing?"

"Just a node and a temporary line." The woman's frown stays stable. She points me to the roof. "Stairs OK?"

Stairs are fine with the skel. Even on low power. Once I'm up, I pull a micro carbon line from Siro's chrome bag and began to set the anchor in the roof. It can't get picked up by birds or blown away by the wind this way. There's too much chance something would snag it if I didn't lay it down carefully and then synch it with the rest of the lines on Tower Seven.

The line can't impact physical elements the way they do in the smart part of the city—nothing smart to talk to here—but it can share data and relay information into the apps in a new way. Just Phở will see a bump in traffic. Other Oldtown stores will too.

Once the anchor's set, I trail the thin line through my fingers all around the building, shivering in the shadow of the tower. Use an epoxy to seal it to the roofline. Then I pop the end of the line with its miniature network drive on the ledge. Line-of-sight for days up here.

Once I have it all up, I register the node with the city using my skel's connection and the Happenstance Overlay. Watch it light up, green. Check.

"There you go," I say to Octavian and Siro.

They don't respond.

Fine by me.

When I'm done with the install, especially once the main line-of-sight is in, I can see the impact hit. Down the street, my park begins to shift slowly, adding a new bench. That motion expands, rippling, so that walkways and thoroughfares begin to smooth around the benches. Soon the whole corner's reconfigured, with seats facing the Phở shop, and people have to change directions to go around.

Inside the pocket park, two parents pause and begin talking. "Good to see you! We should grab lunch." People are stepping outside their circuits. It's working.

My shoulders relax. That should help me with quotas. But I don't want any cred for this.

Even so, my cred's wobbling. I can't get a lock on the value.

Even so, I wave the owner's proffered handshake away. She still uses a manual cred-transfer. "Don't worry about it," I say.

But she's not looking at me. She's looking at a wall just below where the tower meets her building's roof. I can hear the load-bearing-wall beneath it groaning.

That isn't going to be okay with the city. The smart tower is growing down over the three-story again. And the restaurant's wall is going to crack.

"I'll report it." How could this happen with a permit down?

"It's because of your Happenstance," Mrs. Pham says. "The buildings move too fast." She means 'move at all.' They shouldn't be moving. But if they are, it's going to be worse now. Because of the new line.

"Not at all, ma'am. No one would do that if there was a risk." Buildings don't move unless an engineer told them to. I haven't told anyone to move anything.

14% charge. I need to hurry back to Tower One before the sun goes down.

Mrs. Pham's cheeks color a deeper hue. "You think you can make me pay, but you can't!"

"What are you talking about?" Utterly befuddled, low on charge.

I'd refused her offer of a tip.

"Your friends said you'd be by if I didn't pay up. That Happenstance was a two-way street. Have you no empathy?" She's almost crying. "You people always take advantage of the next modifications, the next new everything. But," she points at the wall, "it is breaking us."

The three-story building makes a sound like my skel, groaning under the pressure.

Her wall line begins to sound. "Other business owners, in adjoining buildings." She points. That's a lot of angry faces. All wanting to know what I've done.

What have I done?

Massive fail points stacking up, and meantime my own cred is suddenly thriving again. Outside, people are interacting, everything's got a boost. Big, like Siro said. Only this shop is losing out.

"Pay up? Who said that to you?" The penny drops. "Octavian."

Mrs. Pham shrugs. "We can't prove it . . . he knows we can't."

"Has this happened before?"

"Just rumors."

Furious, I look at the Happenstance overlay. Sure enough, someone's running a hap right on top of us. The building is shifting, grinding into the three-story. I power up to full and throw a hold on the modifications.

It's not entirely legitimate, but technically this is my territory so the map lets me do it. The node I just activated fades and the building stops creaking. The crack stops growing. Mrs. Pham whistles appreciation. "Thank you."

"That shouldn't ever happen." I try to see where the work

originated, but the map's powered down to short range, because my skel's charge can't support a citywide. 3%.

I try to grab Siro on my wraps but I can't get a signal out that way either. Not past tower seven. No links. No coms.

The map has faded to a low-charge grey. The only reason I can connect to anything at all is the line I just planted.

Worse, the skel's slowed to a crawl. I can strip it off, which might make it easier to move at this point, since the joints are all servo-guided, but then I'll have zero support, and no way I could get down the stairs. I doubt I can even ping a cab to take me back to Tower One.

I thought I'd packed the emergency charge cables in Siro's bag, but they aren't there. I'm stuck here, until I can get a charge.

Worse than stuck. Dependent.

I look at the restaurant owner. "I'm afraid I need your help." I hate asking for help. It gives people power over you.

When I let her know what I need, Mrs. Pham shakes her head: No solar, no backup charger.

Nothing that will connect with my skel.

I'm stuck in an Oldtown three story with no power, no sunlight. It's too far to walk to get out of the tower shade. We're losing what light remains anyway.

"But I can make some calls for you," she says. She tries to ping Siro first. No answer.

She calls up to my flat for me on her wall screen. It doesn't connect. She tries again.

By the third try, I'm sitting on the floor, my knees and arms locked up. The friendly face of the tower supervisor appears. "Lane! We've been trying to reach you. There's been a flood at your apartment level."

"What do you mean? Since this morning?"

"We had to clear it out. You're being moved down a few floors."

"Temp quarters?" How many floors? Mrs. Pham's looking at me, trying to overhear.

"Permanent—your lease was up anyway, and with the repairs we're going to have to raise the rent to someone with higher cred. Yours is . . . plummeting. I hope you're all right?" The supervisor's smile doesn't say anything of the sort.

To a shadier floor. And I'd never signed a real lease. The tower just let me and a few other creatives crash there to keep the lights on years ago, then I'd started paying rent. Now the building's popular and I'm not.

"I can up my rent. Not a problem." I liked my flat. And I had cred.

But now the other area businesses are filing complaints and I see he's right. My cred's dropping faster than it rose earlier. Damn.

"We've already got someone lined up. You know him, actually." This time, the supervisor frowns.

"Octavian." Siro, how could you trust the man? This is the worst kind of surprise.

A clatter from beyond the restaurant's kitchens. Mrs. Pham leads out one of the customers, who wears a partial skel on a wrist and shoulder. He holds up a power cord. "Yes?"

Oh yes. "I'll pay you back for the charge." Lucky, this. Very.

Mrs. Pham nods. "You can pay me back by stopping what's happening here—keep our home safe."

Payback. I can do that. I just don't know how, not yet.

When I have enough juice from their wall unit—10%—I open the map once more. The hap to Tower Seven's been made under my name. That's why my cred's heading for the gutter again. Good luck getting any of the other engineers to help me either—this has third rail disaster written all over it.

But I can do one thing. I ping Siro. Leave a message. *:: You need to meet me in Oldtown. I found out what Octavian is doing. You can't do a deal with him! ::*

If Siro's working with Octavian, that will get him down here. If he isn't, that will get them *both* down here.

I pull myself up from where I'd sat down when my skel drained. 13% charge now. Enough to get across to the park, where the sun is finally breaking the treeline just a little. It's risky, but I can charge and watch the shop at the same time. "If anyone comes in, stall them, okay?" Mrs. Pham and the customer both agree.

I sit on the jungle gym, soaking in late afternoon sunlight. When I see Octavian approaching, I drop my first happenstance. Just up the street from where he's walking. A big fountain, ornate hypercarbon, with plenty of water features.

I've been prepping it for an hour, loudly, so that all the search bots lurking in the happenstance grid can alert their owners.

The fountain pushes against the hypercarbon surface of the smart road there at the edge of Oldtown, self-printing and generating more of itself as it goes. Octavian sees the bulge in the street, but doesn't quite understand what it means yet.

The bowl of the fountain hollows out, and from within it, another tier rises, then another. Water begins to trickle down the terraces, catching the light and refracting it.

"Mrs. Pham, I came to check the work done by our engineer," Octavian says.

Our.

There's enough pull on the pipes from that fountain that Civ Engineering is bound to check in. I block their calls. They'll alert the city. The police.

Then I toss my second happenstance, the one that sets off the fire alarms in the lowest three floors of Tower Seven.

The fountain's big enough now that people can sit by it, cool off in the spray.

11% power. The skel's dropping fast. *:: Lane what are you doing? ::* Siro pings. *:: Octavian left like his hair was on fire, and I'm trying to catch up. I saw your haps drop. What happened? ::*

:: I'll show you when you get here. ::

By this time, there are a ton of people in the streets. Those who've begun flocking to my workpoints in hopes of catching some serendipity have come to Oldtown. Dozens of them.

And then the Tower Seven residents emerge because of the alarms.

Octavian's surrounded by people. Happenstance seekers and residents of the old town and the new.

That's when I walk out from the park to meet him.

I unblock the fire department, the city. Connect to a wide-channel for everyone in range, except Octavian. I can network too.

Octavian stares at all the luck seekers.

:: That man's been shaking down your city, charging people for

serendipity. ::

I show them the evidence, and Mrs. Pham comes out to back me up. Several other store owners and residents light up my statement and share it.

With so many people around, when Octavian sees me, he doesn't threaten or try to wave everything off.

"Why didn't you say anything before?" one of the CivEs asks Mrs. Pham. "Someone would have helped you."

"We didn't think anyone would believe us," Mrs. Pham says.

In the crowd, Octavian turns this way and that. "City wants to talk to you," a firefighter says. She waves a hand and two officers take Octavian away.

My skel pings. *:: Your apartment's available again. ::*

Thought it might be.

They send a real lease this time. I'll look it over. Later.

I'm watching the city reps stare at the ornate fountain in the middle of Oldtown. The CivE raises her eyebrows. "Who's going to pay for that?"

The crowd looks at the fountain too. They turn to me and I groan.

My cred, what's left of it, isn't nearly enough to pay for an entire fountain, plus all the water. So much for the loft.

But then Mrs. Pham raises her hand. "I'll help."

"And me," says someone from Tower Seven. Their words echo in the crowd.

More volunteer, until the entire neighborhood has pooled enough cred for the disruptive, ornate Happenstance. I'm amazed. The waterspouts glitter in the refracted light.

Siro finally arrives. The sight of him makes my breath hurt. I keep breathing anyway.

He spots the fountain. "What did you *do*? How did all this happen?"

Mrs. Pham laughs. "Just old fashioned good luck."

By the time my skel's at 100% and I'm ready to leave, Siro and the city have talked up a tentative utility fee rather than privatization.

"You'll stay?" he asks me.

The setting sun passes through the trees, hitting the fountain. The light bubbles and tumbles across the water, sending dappled sunlight across the shadowed alley.

"I will, but I want rights, access. Lockout privileges." I hold my gaze steady as he squirms. "I'll ship you your things."

It's a good kind of change, for the moment. Like all the best surprises.

Fran Wilde's novels and short stories have been finalists for four Nebula Awards, a World Fantasy Award, and two Hugo Awards, and include her Nebula- and Compton-Crook-winning debut novel *Updraft*, its sequels *Cloudbound*, and *Horizon*, her 2019 double-starred Middle Grade novel *Riverland*, and the Nebula-, Hugo-, and Locus-nominated novelette *The Jewel and Her Lapidary*. Her work appears in publications including *The New York Times*, *The Washington Post*, *Asimov's*, *Tor.com*, *Beneath Ceaseless Skies*, *Shimmer*, *Nature*, and *Uncanny Magazine*. She is director of the Genre MFA Concentration at the University of Western Colorado. You can find her at franwilde.net.

"Happenstance" originally appeared in the first volume of *Futurescapes*.

on the nuclear porch,

Hal Y. Zhang

asphalt in our sinuses,
sipping what we cannot
swallow. ghosts announce themselves:
the Tings, family of five.
youngest daughter likes watching
songbirds in her pleated skirt.
it's not about pity, but some kind of
justice. parents do factory work, pipe thickets
to meet our needs until
the accident that is
no accident. it's a feature, the inevitable
explosion when there are so many that stay intact
to pay for the lawsuit. the smoke powers
our lives, our lungs—how to choose one?
how to cast fault on the neighbors, sliced
and diced blocks on pavement with
sincerity, nothing more dangerous. to point fingers
at the designer, the engineer, the architect,
the people for living & breathing closed eyes, the sun
for stinging radiation. blame the ill
for malingering, blame the dead
for standing quiet
for whispers
for pathos
for not fading

Victor St.

Hal Y. Zhang

I remember my first death
under dim lights. A smear of fur
and utter dark on the asphalt,
life stretched and flattened onto the killing plane
described by a singular yellow lamp of
suburban wrongness. I snapped
my neck away, blood-phantom-shard-pain
of seeing something terrible in the sublime.
oof, roadkill, my father said, as if we
should be described by how our murderers
twist the knife. All night I dreamt
of vengeance and the black serrated blade
until I was tugged in by the extended arm of my mother
who did not know the new changeling
in her daughter's body shirking the
garish daylight, helpless to alter our
sun and moon elliptical orbit. Then round the corner
with not-yet-myopic eyes I could see precisely
nothing below new buds of the imprisoned
city pear, midday wheels heaving over
a lacuna blown on the negative reel
of my mind as if maliciously
imagined. I lingered. Here was a
vanished crime scene cleared
of all wrongdoing, not even a televised
sham trial. As my head lightened into her embrace
I could hear my mother's sinewy panic above
all else, a pietà for the unborn
and undeserving.

Hal Y. Zhang is a word arranger and lapsed physicist who splits her time between the east coast of the United States and the Internet. She writes at halyzhang.com, and her science fiction chapbook *Hard Mother, Spider Mother, Soft Mother* was published by Radix Media.

Thank You For Your Patience

Rebecca Campbell

I'm lucky because they replaced a bunch of chairs last month and I got a new one. A good chair is important when you spend ten hours a day in a cubicle talking to strangers about their problems. I've been here three years and worked on most of Westermorgen's services which means I can with no thought help grandma set up her wifi. Or troubleshoot banking software. Or set up your cellphone plan or help you with some app designed to find your soulmate that nevertheless fills you with hopelessness.

(I can't help you with the hopelessness.)

It's nonstandard, but I'm Westermorgen's floater, and Geordie or Keersty just drop me where the calls are heavy or turnover is high. On twitter I can answer questions within five seconds of some asshole in Toronto saying wtf my TV doesn't see the house network. And I respond *I'm sorry to hear that @TOasshole let's see if I can help.* I'm impossible to rile because I've heard everything, every possible stupid question, every strange request regarding lapsed policies and missed payments, every paranoid rant, every sort of impotent rage. The management is shitty and the customers are irritable, but there's beauty in problem solving.

The really bad stuff started at the end of last month, when I had to do a 1-on-1 with Geordie, teamlead for the floor. I'd been fielding a bunch of questions regarding a recent patch that had broken everything. I had this rhythm hitting my 30s AHT and typing without thinking *Mark here how can I help you.* But 1-on-1 is a mandated interruption, so I listened to Geordie brainstorm about improving morale. They stopped having barbecues because it was too expensive even when the burgers were sawdust and soy. Also no one wanted to be outside because Detroit was still burning and the ppm up to something like Beijing.

"Listen to this. Westermorgen. Idol," Geordie told me. "We judge three of the top ranked calls and we have a thing and someone walks away with a Timmy's gift card. Like. Fifty bucks."

Geordie said that like it was a good thing.

"What about a key fob?" I asked. We can't get out without

one after hours, but only management can hold. "Or the winner gets to wear jeans. Or keep their phone for a shift?" That didn't rate an answer. The most frustrating thing about Westermorgen is that teamleads have to hold your phone, like you're an untrustworthy teenager who's been grounded. I feel like I'm lost in a cave or a space station. When I do a lot of overtime I arrive when it's dark and I leave when it's dark and while sometimes I go around the corner for coffee or McNuggets, it always feels like I'm just visiting the world. I don't know what's happened: if a government's fallen, or an ice shelf has collapsed, if Detroit is burning again, or maybe California, or the Great Lakes are dying at a slightly faster rate than they were when I left for work.

Never knowing what's going on outside, I sit in my good chair and say *That sounds frustrating*, to everyone, no matter who's talking or what they want, *let me see if I understand your problem.*

"You could judge," Geordie said, still talking about morale. "You're impartial. You hate everyone."

"I don't hate everyone, Geordie," I said reflexively, though to be fair, I hate a lot of people here.

After my mandated fifteen minutes with Geordie I saw that Misty had a problem with my documentation, which has been rough since they changed policy on me. She's in the Philippines where most of the real work happens. Upper management is all in India. They only have us because they need Canadian accents on the phones, and they get tax breaks, bringing jobs to one of the more desolate parts of the country. Downwind from Detroit, rampant West Nile, and ninety percent of the province's heavy metals processed at the plant out by the mall. Seventy percent of the babies born here are girls, something to do with residual BPA.

Misty is on the other side of the Pacific, in Legazpi, but you'd think she was right here, considering how aggressively she organizes us.

ur shit at filling the forms mark the write up is going to kill ur rank

We're stack ranked every shift. It gets you points you can redeem which, honestly, is worth it for the grocery store gift cards.

Just tell me what I did wrong, Legazpi.

We were in the middle of a rough month. The flu hit everywhere at once and no one could afford to lose the work, so we had a bunch of people come in sick, coughs and juicy sneezes all over the floor, and half the time you got on the elevator and everyone was grey-faced and weaving.

I came in over the weekend to cover mobile because they lost half their staff, so I'd been on for eight days by Monday when Geordie was manic trying to call people in so he wouldn't have to go on phones. He always says, when we're smoking outside and he's pointedly not looking at the place where the GM building used to be, "It's not the extra fifty cents an hour, it's the fact that I don't have to deal with people." He hated taking calls.

He offered me overtime, so I started coming in at six and leaving at ten, and I didn't even notice the weekend. I do remember going home those nights and thinking how hollow my room felt, with my roommates playing CoD in the living room, and how my body seemed to vibrate. Caffeine maybe, or pseudoephedrine. I heard phantom time warnings and chimes, and when I closed my eyes I could see the screen and call after call flooding the queue. By Saturday Westermorgen was a haunted house, but I still wasn't sick.

That sounds frustrating. Let me see if I can help.

I was dealing with this woman on Vancouver Island who couldn't generate invoices. We'd been at it for two hours and I could feel her getting upset when I told her to wipe the whole system and start again. I can help you do that, but she was like no we'll lose two weeks of work, and there's nothing I can say to that, so we keep troubleshooting even though it's pointless.

"Okay, I said, can you go back to the root invoice and try—"

"—oh," she said, "what—"

And that was it, I didn't hear anything but the line itself, which just went dead, that kind of absence you get when someone hangs up on you.

"Are you there? Ma'am?"

I called back but I got a re-order tone, not voicemail or an old-fashioned busy signal but the one that means the whole system is busy or blocked or down.

I dropped out of the queue then, which you're not supposed to do obviously, and went looking for Geordie, who was chatting with Keersty about Westermorgen Idol. I asked if they knew anything but of course they didn't and when I asked if I could at least grab my phone to see what was happening, Keersty did a kind of elementary-school-teacher sigh.

documentation for #3990180 ur overdue mark.

Caller dropped

saw that. explanation?

Happening across the board. Looks like the problem is at their end.

I didn't find out until Mo came back from break streaked wet in the way you are if you've run out into that rain blowing in from Detroit because you don't want it to touch your skin, saying, "Earthquake on the westcoast. You know anyone out there?"

I thought about the woman trying to get the invoice together for a tiny order of sea salt from some equally tiny place on Vancouver Island, her business so miniscule it all fit into our cheapest subscription. In my un-submitted documentation for Misty I had written that her voice sounded like a hopeful-but-slightly-overwhelmed Great Aunt trying to make the remote control work.

"No one. How bad?"

"Like 9.6. The worst since forever. For hundreds of years."

"Jesus," I said, "Jesus. Jesus."

I've had similar moments on calls. When the shooting happened in Montreal—not Vieux-Montreal, but the one where the kids ran downtown away from McGill, and the photographer caught the girl as the bullet tore out her right kneecap—I was on the line with this dickwad in a coworking space on Maisonneuve who was asking to talk to my supervisor. Then—mid whine—he stopped talking, like he suddenly didn't care about my attitude. I could hear his phone pinging.

"Sir, are you there?"

"Can you hear that? It's happening on the street. I can see—"

A faint popping. Voices raised and doors slammed. Then he cut the call.

I kept in the queue. I helped someone update. I did a subscription renewal. The next person, though, needed a backup and that took forever so we chatted about hockey until she said, "Did you hear about Montreal?"

"No ma'am," I said, thinking about that sound I maybe heard before his phone cut. Fire crackers. Backfires.

"Some guys shot up the whole downtown. I think it was terrorists. Who knows. FLQ? Or Muslims maybe. Red Power. Fifty dead but it was going up every time I refreshed the page."

She kept going on like this while we did a backup and then I made sure everything worked and it had been like three hours at that point, and I kept thinking of the guy and his silence, and what was going on in the streets while we talked about his login and how unprofessional I was. I don't have any friends in Montreal. I went there once to drink when I was eighteen, but that's it. I just had that guy and the thump of footsteps fleeing the co-working space.

When I took my break the rain was falling again, the faintly grey kind that runs down the sidewalks and the gutters and when it builds up enough you can see that it's a little milky because it's full of ash. If you think too hard about what's running into your eyes as you stand outside, smoking until your pack is empty, you go eat a twenty-four box of Tim Bits, or six Big Macs, or you stop for one beer on the way home and only leave when they push you out the door.

Geordie was outside. I gave him a cigarette even though he doesn't smoke, either, and he said, "it doesn't seem to be getting cleaner. Wasn't it supposed to get cleaner?" He grew up in Detroit, though he was already over here when it burned last year.

"Maybe it's safer. The hum is worse. I thought the hum was supposed to go when they sent in the cleanup crews."

We watched the warm, ash-coloured water run down the gutters until it was ankle deep. The city is a wetland, and there isn't far for water to go, so it ends up in people's basements, all that ashy, bony water running through foundations and drains, a constant trickle in the background. Sort of like the faint pop you might hear while you're on the phone with a guy in Montreal who wants to talk to your manager.

"Does it feel." Geordie said and lit another cigarette.

"What, Geordie." I hate how often he doesn't finish his sentences.

"Does it feel like it's happening more often? This kind of thing?"

I dropped my smoke into the rain water and shrugged, then said, "I wish I knew what to tell you." Which wasn't a real answer, and I used my tech support voice when I said it because I didn't want to have that conversation.

On my first break after the earthquake I smoked and watched the rain and videos on my phone, someone livestreaming the moment it hit—boring talk about food or weather, then a strange look on their face, their eyes dart upward, then the phone falls. Overhead footage from helicopters of downtown Vancouver, all those green towers swaying and falling, and the bridge swinging until the cables snap like rubber bands. The worst in recorded history. Worse, probably, than the last megathrust in 1700. I just kept thinking of that woman, and the sort of quiet shock in her voice, her "oh—is that—" and then nothing, and I was standing out in the rain, but still warm, when it occurred to me that I might have heard her last words. I kept thinking about the texture of the silence after the call dropped and what had happened the moment after that, if that had been the worst of it, the shock of the whole world rumbling. Or if it had been worse for her after that, or right now, or tomorrow.

I only had ten minutes because call volume was increasing. My throat was starting to tickle, and the world—just suddenly, out of nowhere—started to look glassy, the light thick from the ceiling squares, and my skin prickled when I ran my hands over my arms, which were covered with goose bumps.

The floor was nearly empty except for Geordie running around supervising and not taking calls, and the queue was packed. My first call was from way north along the coast, Prince Rupert, a woman calling about a password reset. "I want Mark," she said, "He helped me before. Can I talk to Mark?"

While I was documenting I thought, fuck it, I'm going to tell Misty what the woman told me while we were waiting for the password reset email, about how when you're that far north you don't notice time passing, and you feel good in an unimaginable way in summer, luminous and hopeful, and how in winter all you want to do is die and drink yourself into a coma, so you know, it balances out.

After that I reopened #3990180.

An elderly woman, I wrote, *on a phone, trying to print invoices for locally produced sea salt, looks over at the rack of glass jars in which she keeps her stock because she hears a rattle, then another, then she says, "oh—is that—" and nothing else because at that moment, the force of twenty-five thousand Hiroshimas lit the Cascadia subduction zone—on which Vancouver island rests like a cork on a bottle—centuries of continental tension released.*

I typed that, then I hit send, then I added a secondary note on her file. *At 8.32 PST a 9.8 hit the Cascadia subduction zone.*

And Misty was right there on ChatHive, not telling me it was Inappropriate. She wrote, *rest their souls* and I was comforted by those temporary words, which surprised me.

my grandparents were on mindanao in the 1976 earthquake. u got anyone there?

No

I heard the hum from Detroit. It was, somehow, a relief to know that across the world Misty was in a similar room among people evaluating documentation for apps and ISPs and accounting software. People saying *that must be frustrating, let's see if I can help.* Something occurred to me.

You hear anything about tsunamis?

no word so far

Do you have your phone? So you can get the alerts?

theyll let us know. we're so bad im taking calls so i won't be fixing ur doc until tomorrow

I wondered if Keersty would let us know, or if she would dither about it until all we could do was climb to the top floor of the building and watch a wave consume what was left of Detroit before it swamped us, too.

Five more calls and I refilled my water bottle—the one with the slogan on it, *fueling small business with the tools to succeed*, that some now-lost Westermorgen contract brought in—and I was looking at my skin reflected in the sink, which was the colour of those pale, lumpy smokers you see outside the entrance, the colour of a raw filet o fish. I felt adrenalized, like a moment before I'd been terrified, but I could not remember how or why. I wondered what it was doing to me, inside, all those cells now remade into virus factories, turning to goo and mush and sloughing off while the virus proliferated through my system, and I left traces on everything I touched.

The water ran over the top of the bottle. Clear. So far the ash hasn't worked its way through the city's water system. Or maybe it had and it was invisible like the microplastics in the lake.

"So you going to judge?" It was Geordie. "We're going to do it next week. I was thinking we'd set a time limit. Like, five minute calls. You and me and Keersty judge it. I grabbed fifty for the Timmy's card, too."

"Man," I said, "man."

Geordie just stared at me. "You getting sick? You know what you need to do is . . . ." He went on about Echinacea or FluFX and I thought about the tsunami that was, or was not, traveling across the Pacific. ". . . Or just hammer your system with anti-oxidants, and take a double dose of Nyquil—"

Without thinking I pulled my phone out of my pocket.

"—You know you can't have that anywhere near the floor."

I was already googling Pacific tsunami alert, and it was rolling rainbows and I stared at it so hard that it seemed to take over the whole world, and then I shivered, but Geordie was still talking.

"Don't make me write you up. I don't want to deal with it."

"K." I said.

"It's about privacy for our users. They need to know they can trust our integrity, our word, and our system."

The poster on the far side of the break room said *Integrity, Word,* and *System.* I saw that the alert had been issued for Japan. That's when he took my phone.

"You fuck the dog, I have to write you up. I don't want to write you up."

Japan in six hours. Eight pm. I'd still be here, while very far away a wave crested on the seacoast, filling the river basins and the car parks.

I know you don't have to surrender your phone, even if they can require you to leave it at home. I know they're not supposed to lock you in, either, or let you smoke within three metres of the door, even when the ash is falling. They're not supposed to pay you in points you can then exchange for grocery store gift cards, which you need because the new minimum wage doesn't even cover rent. But I need a job.

The next call I got was farther south, closer to the epicenter. The first thing I did was ask about the earthquake.

"We felt it, and there's the tsunami warning, but we're far enough inland it shouldn't be—"

"—Tsunami warning?"

"So when I try to log in—"

"—Tsunami?"

"—I keep getting the same error, it says my account's frozen. What does that mean? I need to do some invoices. And yeah, I just got the text like half an hour ago. Landfall is like an hour."

The account was frozen due to missed payments, so I pointed that out and the guy insisted no, he'd set up an automated transfer, and he kept me on the line while he chatted with the bank's tech support on another line to sort out the direct deposit, and then I reactivated his account, all this time the tsunami traveling toward the coast, where the shallower bottom would raise the wave's height by narrowing its length because the last time I'd been outside I'd looked at a gif on Wikipedia that demonstrated how tsunamis crest as they travel through shallow waters.

The last thing he said wasn't *thanks*, it was "there it is, the tide's going way out, I hope everyone's out of downtown." Then he was gone, and I could imagine it, the water running away from shore, like a huge exhalation, and then collecting into a rising wave that would destroy them all.

The tsunami warning? I wrote in ChatHive, hoping Misty was there.

Keersty responded instantly: *That is not appropriate ChatHive is for important work stuff.*

we havent heatd anything but were swamped so who knows what going on outside

CHATHIVE CHANNEL WILL ONLY BE USED FOR APPRORPAITE BUSINESS RELATED BUSINESS.

Maybe you should get out anyway.

CHATHIVE CHANNEL WILL ONLY BE USED FOR

APPRORPAITE BUSINESS RELATED BUSINESS.

CHATHIVE CHANNEL WILL ONLY BE USED FOR APPRORPAITE BUSINESS RELATED BUSINESS.

I'd been there for sixteen hours, and I couldn't remember the last time I slept a full night at home, when I hadn't been buzzed on cold pills and exhaustion, and the sound of CoD from the living room. That week when I did sleep I kept saying *This is Mark from Magnacorp* or *This is Mark from Wherever I Am Right Now,* and heard explosions and the way voices carry over the river from Detroit, the screams and the crowds and the gunshots. Or maybe I was never actually asleep, maybe I was just off my head. I shouldn't have washed the pills down with beer, but there's that thing that happens when you stop in for a beer after work and the inertia of the whole thing, the job, the shitty beer and the fact that a person brings you food, even if you can't afford it, that sticks you to your seat. It was bad last summer when we couldn't afford to run the AC but the bar on the way home could, and it was full of familiar guys, broke and lonely and trying to avoid looking at what was left of the Detroit skyline, or the grey-green clouds boiling to the north, and the hail and the lightning storms every afternoon like clockwork. The summers are definitely hotter, and the mosquitoes are definitely worse, and last summer I noticed that the birds don't sing anymore, all their whistles sound like videogame lasers.

I stepped outside for a cigarette and realized the doors had been locked and I don't have a fob because I don't rate a fob. Geordie was there too, setting up his stupid Westermorgen Idol, piles of bright pink and green and blue post-it notes all over his desk.

"I need to go out."

"The doors are locked for the night."

"I need to get out."

"We lost another girl from Online. You'll have to take over social media if we lose anyone else. Take your break here."

I just kind of stared at him and my skin prickled like all the pseudoephedrine I'd taken had rushed to the surface and was blasting every single nerve ending in my body.

"I need to go outside."

"You *can't.* Like, you physically can't."

I kind of stood there and I'm ashamed to say I wanted to cry. Like a little kid who isn't allowed to use the bathroom, or who just wants to sit with his Dad but keeps getting dragged away by unfamiliar relatives. The kind of crying you see on the bus at rush hour when some little kid coming back from the mall loses it and lies in the aisle wailing, cramming road salt in his mouth, and you just think *you and me both.*

I didn't actually cry. I hate myself, because I just said, begging, "can I please can I have my phone back, please?"

Geordie looked at me like I was an idiot, him in the middle of all the post-it notes that read CONGRATULATIONS! or YOUR A WINNER! or WESTERMORGEN IDOL!!!

I didn't say anything. I left. At first I just sat in the lunch room, shivering and nauseous, staring at a plastic solo cup leftover from the barbecues they used to give before the ash. There will be worse moments in my life no doubt—more pain, more sadness—but I can't imagine anything so wide-ranging in its desolation as that moment. The only thing I could focus on was telling Misty to get her phone back and watch the horizon and be ready to escape.

A girl from Online staggered through, sweaty and pale, and I knew that Geordie would be here in a moment to ask for another eight hours, overnight, answering strangers' questions so perfectly that they all treat me like a shitty customer service AI built to serve.

There aren't a lot of choices in your life, are there? You can choose to have kids, or not, or leave your hometown or not. Or to stay in a terrible job you are, for some reason, very good at. But other than that, what is there? Just a lot of compliance and noncompliance. This didn't feel like a choice. I said to the girl, "we need to get out of here," and she nodded. Then we headed down to the lobby. The doors were locked and no one carrying a key was in the building and the girl looked bad, but when I went to the fire escape she still said, "no, we're not supposed to!"

"We need to get out—"

"—they'll *fire* us!" And I could hear the fear in her voice, and I wondered how badly she needed this job, that she was here in the middle of the night, so sick she could hardly stand.

"Tell them I did it," I said, and hit the bar.

Only it didn't move because it was locked, too. The next thing I did was stupid, but I don't know what else I could have done. I walked back to the lobby and picked up a garbage can and began slamming it into the glass door. Behind me she was just coughing and coughing and said, maybe, "stop stop," but so faintly I could ignore it. Then we were out, and she was staggering toward the emergency room on Ouellette and I was alone in rainwater the same temperature as my blood. Then I went looking for a payphone because the only way to sort this out was to call in, but I couldn't remember which of Westermorgen's departments Misty was assigned to so when I finally found the city's last payphone—in the bus depot—I called them all, all the sad voices of men and women here and on the other side of the world.

"Welcome to Caiphas Business Systems, Jane speaking, how can I help you?" "Welcome to Tesla Mobility, how can I help you?" "Welcome to Roscommon Account Services." "Welcome to Lighthouse Mobility."

"I'm looking for Misty. She helped me before."

"I'm sure I can help you. What's your user number?"

"Misty. Misty knows," I said, my voice querulous and elderly. "Put on Misty!"

I could hear the exhaustion in his silence, then the compliance. "One moment, and I'll transfer you."

"Hey Misty." I said, "Misty. Misty. You need to get to high ground."

"What? Who is this?"

"Just promise, k?"

"There's no tsunami warning—"

"—it's on its way. It's passing Japan and Hawaii. It hit the Aleutians. California." I hoped she didn't mistake me for what I felt like, right then: a crazy old man, mad with loneliness, longing to hear a voice in the void, even if it was only to harangue them for the weakness of their service and the terrible nature of their product.

"Mark?"

"Another six hours to landfall. I know you'll still be on shift. Promise."

I waited for her to disconnect, which was okay because at least I'd told her. Then I think maybe she said, "Thank you, Mark," or maybe it was just the noise in my head. I held the line another moment, then hung up. I felt okay because I'd got through, because I wasn't in a cubicle anymore, because I could walk home and enjoy the silence before CoD marathons in the living room, enjoy the ashy rain falling across my slowly cooking skin.

I walked home hoping Misty said, "thank you, Mark." It felt like I was slipping through a gap in the world, between noises, a kind of silent passage, the way kids slip along the abandoned rail easements in town, below grade, the corridors of grass and rats and squirrels and birds. Between the noise of the phones and CoD. Between heartbeats. Between cresting waves, the silence you hang onto for just a moment when someone hangs up, before you go onto the next call because there is, temporarily, a respite from the tyranny of the queue. The silence after a bullet connects, or a wave hits on the other side of the world. I just hoped, harder and harder and harder, that Misty would insist they unlock the doors and break the windows and they could escape before the wave arrived to wash the rest of us away.

Rebecca Campbell is a Canadian writer and teacher. Her work has appeared in *The Magazine of Fantasy and Science Fiction*, *Clarkesworld*, and *Interzone*, as well as other magazines and anthologies. NeWest Press published her first novel, *The Paradise Engine*, in 2013. You can find her online at whereishere.ca.

Sky Suck

Juliana Roth

They hired me last Sunday to suck the carbon from the sky. I imagined the job might give my writing wings; I'd fly across the lower atmosphere with a vacuum strapped to my back like a forgotten character from the *Ghostbusters* franchise. But it turns out to be nothing like that. I was given the job mostly because my pilot's license is still valid from the war.

Lee, the chief engineer, leads me to my plane. It's nothing more than a small Turboprop a billionaire might take to an island off of what's left of Belize, but she promises the plane has the propulsion potential of a spacecraft. "When you near a highly concentrated carbon pocket, the plane might shake a bit. The carbon is sequestered in an inner chamber filled with a high concentration of photosynthetic algae. There's a photoelectric cell submerged in the water tank and a simulation of sunlight to drive the photosynthesis process. The outburst of oxygen propels you, once you get to a high enough altitude."

"I could run out of carbon?"

Lee stifles a laugh at my question. "There's an endless supply of carbon. We are beyond capacity. Your shift will be over long before the carbon concentration in an area drops to a level that will no longer sustain you. You are there to clean the sky."

The tropical storm that wiped out the eastern Antilles only took three hours to move up in classification to a category six hurricane. It was the second to touch down after they added the new classification when Florida was swept up by 200 mph winds. Unheard of, but not unimaginable. We'd known where our weather patterns were headed for years, but people just raised their homes up on stilts and went on living their lives. Not that I blame them. Not that I'd want to move if there seemed to be a way to keep my life going with some normalcy if I could, but then again I haven't lived anywhere for more than four months at a time since I left college.

I thought I was going to be a screenwriter before I got drafted. I bought pink sheets and a *Breakfast at Tiffany's* eye mask I wore to bed each night. I thought this was the way you brought Hollywood to you, making routines in your life like you were already there.

I also had the idea you needed to work at a coffee shop at some point in your life to really be considered a writer. I jumped from coffee shop to coffee shop, but the same thing happened in every city I worked in: the workforce's disposable income dropped, the cost of milk skyrocketed as dairy farmland dried up, a shipment of coffee beans from South America was blown up by a local militia, and the coffee shop closed up. I barely had enough time to get the down-on-my-luck-service-job experience I needed to become the writer I knew I could be before I had to find my way to another city and another open barista position. I felt like I had stumbled into my destiny, like finding those jobs was a sign I was headed in the right direction.

After I got my letter, I went to a psychic. It turned out to be the best thing I ever did for myself. I had the draft notice in my pocket as I sat across from her. I closed my eyes and shuffled the tarot deck like she told me to, letting the cards dance between my hands until something inside of me told me to stop. I hadn't been around anyone before who honored that there might be something inside of you like that, never met someone who told you to follow that something.

I'd thought being a screenwriter and storyboarding in a room full of writers might be like that. Someone might laugh and riff off of a joke I'd written over the weekend as I sipped my soy latte at the corner of a coffee shop hunched over a worn notepad. But in wartime there's no time left for dreams, and when the war is with the environment, dreams evaporate all at once. I smiled at the psychic as she took the deck back and pulled the first card, then another, lining them around the table into a cross.

"You are being called to an adventure, but not the one you'd thought you'd be going on. What you needed from the one you imagined you will find in the other instead." A story by credit? An enticing character arc to really nail my studio pitch?

The psychic went on to say I was heartbroken and some other things I already knew about myself, like that I had a bad relationship with my sister. I left the shop thinking over what she'd said about my adventure, and I started to feel ripped off—not by her, but by the world. Who chooses war over being in a writer's room? I certainly didn't. I didn't make a choice at all. And there was nothing to be done about my sister. She'd died the year before in an apartment fire set off by thermal radiation when a misfired hydrofracking blast triggered an earthquake, the tremors cracking a nuclear reactor three miles from her apartment in Lawrence County, Pennsylvania. Her name was Sally Fisher. You can look all of this up.

You'd be right to think there were disasters happening everywhere. I didn't have anyone to give my new bed sheets to when I was deployed, so I donated them, but I kept the eye mask. I thought it might come in handy.

I don't remember much of my time as a pilot, based in Mexico, flying missions in South America. I spent several days a week in the shade of a canvas tent working on a spec script for *The Simpsons* in between my rations of bread and coffee. Sometimes I put my eye mask on and took a nap. The other soldiers were rarely around. I was the only pilot stationed there and essentially my own boss.

Usually, by mid-week, I was handed a map with coordinates. I'd enter them into the GPS system on my plane and take off for a few days, following my new adventure just like the psychic said. A cloud might look briefly beautiful, and I took comfort in this. When the GPS began to beep, I pushed my thumb against the thick red button to drop a bomb on whatever local militia was siphoning off water from a town's water tank or committing some other infraction against the AGAST (Allies for the Global Alleviation of Storm Trauma) treaty.

I returned to what was left of the United States three years ago, and since then the sky has become more dangerous. The carbon particles that trap heat in the atmosphere are transparent, so it's hard to measure in real-time what I suck up, Lee tells me. Most of the aerosols that make it difficult to see were artificially introduced by AGAST to bounce the light from the sun back up into space, going against decades of advocacy to clean the soot and sulfur from the sky. To simultaneously clean up the carbon and replace it with aerosols was the best they could come up with to try to stabilize the heat, but it's only time before the next storm hits. Now AGAST is working on a proposal to mandate breathing filters for at-risk elevations.

Lee mentions that the pilot I'm replacing had an asthma attack last week before boarding the plane and hasn't returned since. This doesn't bother me the way it might have years ago. Death feels bureautic these days, more like the outcome of an assembly line than anything a god or enemy might've done to you in an era where death could be more creative, more Shakespearean. I've stopped mourning who I've lost, what I've lost, the Earth itself. The only thing I can't let go of is my desire to see a story of mine told. I know the studio systems have long gone under, and book publishers shut down, but I keep writing with an overwhelming sense that my chance is just around the corner.

When Lee starts up the plane, the exhaust pipe coughs out what looks like a chunk of artificial particles. This is what's meant to save us? I kick the piece of strange coal around before getting in the pilot's seat. The dusty handprint of the former pilot is still on the door. Alarmed, Lee wipes this away and stands proudly, opening up the door.

"Go ahead," she says, smiling. "It's all yours."

A multi-genre writer and educator raised in Nyack, NY, Juliana Roth is the creator of the narrative web series, The University, which follows the bureaucratic failures of a university in the aftermath of a sexual assault on campus. Juliana worked in programming and communications for the Ecology Center, the Center for the Education of Women, and the World Animal Awareness Society. Her writing has appeared or is forthcoming in *Entropy*, *VIDA Review*, *Irish Pages*, *The Atticus Review*, *The Establishment*, *Yemassee*, among other publications. Currently, she is a Publishing Fellow with the Los Angeles Review of Books at the University of Southern California. You can find her here: www.julianaroth.com

PLANÈTE
(ET L'HUMANITÉ)

After Erysichthon

Kaye Boesme

The whole world is a feast of runaway craving,
of a curse that has outrun its uses.
Early on, our ancestors twisted up,
moved root through rock, spread fragile first leaves wide.
All land was new, mountainous, unsoiled.

The forests that grew have lasted so long,
spreading across the world at glacial pace.
We stretch and recede, grow up and move out.
Famine and war will parch your lips, drag you
below the Earth where we feast on your flesh.

What is breath but the ambrosia of trees?
You suckle our gaseous exhalations.
We wean you down to Hades at your death.

Who are these children who warm,
strain, and devour the wide earth,
cornucopia fraying,
desert bursting at its seams?

We are the trees who were once never wronged,
not axe-culled, not forced to grow through fences.
The Thunderer and those bright kin alone
touched us, burned us, but we claimed the wide land.
Forgotten myths say we gave birth to you.

We danced with Hermes on sloping mountains,
later with Pan whom my tall sister bore.
To me came Artemis' strict retinue.
We ran in those places no man dared see.
Then your people grew up and tamed the wilds.

The gifts we brought you at your birth were myrrh,

frankincense, and storax, life-giving scents
beloved of gods, the sweat from our bark.

Erysichthon was condemned
as he felled that first grove.
Its nymph guardian begged, and
sap pooled at her feet like blood.

Forests fell back, expanding horizons.
When we seduced you, we brought you to groves,
breathed in the incense and breath you exhaled,
taught you secrets of bees and bitter plants.
You worshipped us alongside stone statues.

We know which of you swung the axe to cut
deep into the sap-giving arteries,
your grandmothers and sisters cut to stumps.
This is how we learned how to give curses.
Now all-consuming hunger binds us all.

Persephone opens wide arms to those
initiated into mysteries
shining like white cypress bark and gold leaves.

We punish with a hunger.
That murderer devoured
until he bit down deep on
his own tender flesh, ripped hard.

Our lives stretch so long that none can compare.
Curses work best when exercised lightly.
Torchers of nymphs, bearers of distress, you
smashed so many of us, pried open trunks,
carved once-sacred wood to ford the wide sea.

Rage boils thick in our sap when nymphs die.
We witness trunks uprooted, roots twisted
hard from a fall driven by gravity.
More often, they're intact, dead from disease.

Dryads decay hidden in scrapped branches.

What you give the forest opens the way.
Here in mountain places, philosophers
found pathways in sunbeams mottled with green.

The hexed consume without end,
now without limit or death.
Their tools extract Plouton's wealth;
all the world weeps out poison.

In perfumed shrines where our secret teachings
saturated air, ground, and cool water,
offerings blackened cave ceilings with soot.
We cannot suckle those who have breath, not
until your hearts root down in awe of place.

Make white cakes covered in sticky honey.
Go to the chamber of the ones who dwell
among the countless wronged dead, they who howl,
who listen to sapless whispers of shades.
Pacify them and be made whole again.

Come to the mountain, come to the gorge-nook.
The water we pull up through our roots tastes
sweet of nectar and metal, wilds and waste.

We repeat the dead ones' names.
This world is old, the list great,
our curses worn like old silt.

We watch all in reflections
metal and glass leave, your eyes
searching, tamed lightning your guide.

You linger in pallid storefront lights, dark
patterns ghosting across your distracted
faces, forest yet close. Look up. See us.

Sooner or later, your meandering
steps will remember sacred rites once more.
Sooner or later, emptiness will tire
you—you will reach for the wholeness of yore.

Kaye Boesme is a poet, conlanger, and writer. Her poetry has appeared in *Kaleidotrope*, *Illumen*, and *Eternal Haunted Summer*, and she has a short story out in *The Society of Misfit Stories Presents*. More information about her work is available at kayeboesme.com, and she's on Twitter as @kayeboesme. Boesme has a background in library and information science, so while she did not set out to know strange things, strangeness happened upon her.

Ambient and Isolated Effects of Fine Particulate Matter

Emery Robin

On Thursday the sun rose red and stayed red, and stared at us red and red through the shifting candlewax layers of sky. We sealed the windows and cancelled gym, and forbade the children to leave until their mothers came for them, and through lunch period they pressed their noses to the glass and left smears of rainbow oils there. Before their faces and ours the bloody halo crept through the silhouettes of our buildings, picking its way down the foothills, stealing hot and infected towards the wide soft swathe of nothing that had once been San Francisco.

In the early afternoon the children left in bunches and tangles, clusters of heaving minivans like lifeboats. We gathered in the teacher's lounge and stood with our hands wrapped round our one o'clock coffee mugs and said quietly to each other and ourselves the air quality numbers in the neighborhoods to which we would be driving through the greyness: Montclair and Emeryville, San Antonio and El Cerrito, one-eighty-five, two-seventeen, two-fifty, two seventy-one.

Some of us had masks, and some did not. Some had the wrong masks—the flimsy kind, thin and cotton, with no wires at the top to mold over our noses and cheekbones—and we discarded these in the wastebasket, a growing pile of white leaves. Those who did have the right masks put them on and looked at the others with invisible mouths, invisible lips. There were no spares.

The school was a good school. The neighborhood was a good neighborhood. It was in the Oakland hills, and it perched over the Oakland flatlands, their density and cement and graffiti and barred windows, like a pale and decorous vulture. On its borders there was a cemetery, and the cemetery was Oakland writ small: the graves dappled down the hill, and at the top were great marble monuments, pyramids and temples and fountains, and at the bottom flat stones sunk into the grass. As children we had come to these stones and sat upon them and had picnics for our birthday parties. We had stared up at the angels of the rich, and they had stared sightlessly down at us. Beneath them, we had wondered, were the rich staring, too?

Now we stood by our cars in the teachers' parking lot and prepared to pour ourselves down the stooped hills and into the low concrete mazes we called home. Our phones were already alight with emails: would the children have school tomorrow? Would they have school next week? Would they be allowed to re-take their tests, re-write their essays, would there be extra credit? We drove through the grey and the deep grey shadows of the trees. Surely, wrote the parents, even if the district forbade the schools to open, the SAT preparation night would not be cancelled? The college essay preparation night would not be cancelled? Through the dust gathering on our windshields we watched the streetlights shudder into life ahead of us. They knew the property values of this good neighborhood, the parents did not say. They knew the price of this good school.

We sat at our kitchen tables and listened to our husbands read to us in rough voices news articles about what had happened in Paradise. Fathers had run back through fire for their daughters. Families had stood by the side of the road praying for their cars to start up again with the heat beating at their faces. Dogs had survived, and not survived. We closed our eyes and tried to see it, but there was nothing behind our eyelids, only colorlessness.

On Friday the schools were closed all day. Those of us with masks pulled them on and walked out to buy bread, and fruit, and fish for dinner. Some of us hovered in the grocery store by the tall white shelves of bottled water; the great drought was a memory less than a year old. Many of us still had buckets under the faucets in our bathtubs, so that nothing should be wasted. In the grocery store we looked at the water and saw the plastic, stacks and stacks of it like shark's teeth, cylinders huddled together, as if the water were afraid of loneliness and afraid of touching. Those of us without masks stayed home.

The parents began to write new emails: they would not be coming to the college essay night, they said. They would not be coming to the SAT preparation night. Their lungs were weak. Their chests hurt. They had been getting over a cold; now, they could not get over it. They could not breathe. They could not breathe. They could not breathe.

They were leaving Oakland, the parents said. They were driving to their cabins in the mountains. Some of their children were coming with them; others were staying behind. They would return when the air was clear. They would return, once the fire had ended. They would come back to the city once it had made itself clean.

Many of these families had cabins in the mountains. They would ski there in the winter and swim there in the summer. This was the great mountain range on which storms broke and died, the mountain range that had made a desert of Nevada and Utah when the world was younger; these were the mountains in which the Donner Party had sat under snow and ice and eaten the meat from each other's bones. They were covered in blue lakes and green forests. If you walked into these forests, late at night, you could look up and see the whole Milky Way spilling herself from horizon to horizon, under billions of miles of clear and shuddering sky.

Whereas it was not possible to do this in Oakland even before the fire.

The newscasters began to ask when the smoke would clear. For each other they had no answer. The fire, it seemed, would need to die, or the wind would need to change; no scientist knew when either event would come. They cut to their reporters, wide-eyed young women mouthing muffled news through their own masks in front of a blurred horizon. The cool red circle of the sun stared at us through the television.

Schools were closed again all next week. The district told us they would open after Thanksgiving, regardless of air quality. The children could not miss school forever, said the district. We hunched into ourselves over our laptops at our kitchen tables and shuffled and re-shuffled our lesson plans. We walked up the avenues to run errands and ducked into buildings softened to haze. Beside and behind us moved the people of the city, their faces wrapped in blue masks. When they held the doors of BART trains for us and counted dimes and quarters next to us and put our groceries in paper bags their hands were deep brown and tan, scarred and freckled and wrinkled and calloused, but their faces were all paper-blue, pastel blue, as blue as the sky.

Beside the BART station a woman sat down on the ground and began to cough. A crowd gathered around her almost immediately, a clot in the streetflow, and watched her cough until her inhales rasped and sizzled. One of us asked if anyone had called a doctor. The woman said, in between coughs, that no one should call a doctor. She would be healthier without a bill, she said. We watched her until the light changed, and then we dissolved into passers-by, pushing beside her, through her. The smoke hung heavy overhead, and the train roared above like thunder.

The classrooms were emptier on Monday, and the students' voices sounded too loud inside them. They did not seem to wish to speak. When we asked them questions, their answers trailed off into silence. When it was time for gym class, they ran laps around the inside of the theater, the only noise their sneakers thumping over the red carpet, up onto the creaking stage. It took us nearly half the period to realize two boys had gone missing; when we went to look, we found them on the lawn above the library, looking down the hill from which the previous month they had been able to see the whole San Francisco Bay. One of them was holding a joint in his hand; as we came up behind them, he dropped it, unlit, and began coughing hoarse and wispy into his elbow. Half an hour later, when his mother had appeared at the gates in her minivan with her face tight and plastic and afraid, he had still not stopped coughing.

The smoke began to press closer. The sky began to settle lower each morning. It had been difficult to see down the hill; now, it became difficult to see across the street. We woke each morning to a fine layer of grey on our cars, on our lawns. If we stood outside long enough, we found ourselves shaking grey out of our hair. The older women among us told jokes about old age; the younger ones said nothing, but cut their hair short, so that in the thick tangles of their ponytails and braids and curls the colorlessness no longer collected so clearly.

We wondered if the students would ask about this. Some of us even prepared lectures on the topic, clinical or comforting, biological or historical or philosophical, depending on our fields of expertise. But the students were coming to school less, now, joining their parents far from the city in tens and twenties. Those families without houses in the mountains continued to email us, more frantic each day. The district would cancel school again, they said. The district had cancelled girls' tennis, and football. The district did not know when the fire would end. What was our plan for the children to keep their GPAs? What was our plan for the children to keep their scholarships?

Some of us, the ones who lived near enough to the good school in the good neighborhood, took the bus home. On the bus, we began to notice, the people sitting next to us had grey in them. On their hair, in their clothes, of course, like us; but also not like us. The skin of their hands was grey, and their eyes were grey above their masks. They said nothing to anyone—not the bus driver, not the teenage boys shouting dirty things from across the aisle, not the tired-eyed woman asking them for money. None of us saw the grey people leave the bus; our stops always seemed to come before theirs did. We did not mention the grey people to each other. We did not even mention them to our husbands. But we did not forget the way they looked, how they stared at the city rushing by out the window, as if it were invisible, as if there were nothing there at all.

The parents, from their cabins in the mountains, posted photos of the tall frosted pine trees, of their sons or daughters skating out onto mirrored lakes. In these photos the sun was yellow. The light it cast was as white as the snow.

It became difficult to see across a room. It became difficult to see our hands in front of our faces. We drove to school with our headlights on and watched the soft dust fall onto our windshields. In the teachers' lounge we took to grading essays in brighter and brighter colors: purple, green, pink sparkling gel pen, as if we were the teenage girls we had once been. It did not seem to matter. We picked up each piece of paper when we were done and shook it, and watched the ash on it settle to the carpet. The writing below was empty of all color. Even the black printed ink was faded, as if it had been sitting in a room forgotten for many years.

That weekend, one of us had a date, a concert in San Francisco. We wished her luck. The local news did not report from San Francisco any more; sometimes they would drive out to Treasure Island and turn their cameras west, and we would watch the lights of the Salesforce Tower, visible through the haze for a few silent seconds and then gone again. No one had seen Coit Tower since the fire began. There was no word from the tech companies, though we sometimes still saw their buses, employees-only, easing slowly down the streets from our homes towards the South Bay. We saw no one at their windows; but then again, we never had.

A student who we had thought long-gone, one of the earliest to flee to the mountains, showed up in school on Wednesday. We said nothing to her, but we wondered: her face had gone pale as chalk. When she was asked a direct question, she answered in a voice so soft no one could hear her. One of us, who had advised her on her college essay and who knew something of her troubles at home, went to go find her during lunch. She was not sitting with her usual friends, who were huddled on the curled brown lawn slipping bites of sandwiches under their masks. She was standing by the gates, staring at the red eye of the sun. She was not moving. She was not wearing a mask. She was breathing slowly, shallowly, and the grey had settled into her eyelashes and the folds of her coat.

The woman who had gone into San Francisco did not come to school. When we called her cell phone, there was no answer; not even her answering machine picked up. Instead, there was a thin, rustling static, which, when we listened closely, sounded almost like voices.

That night, watching the news from New York and Washington, we did not recognize the sun in the sky behind the newscasters. It was not that it was yellow, or that its light was clear and good. It was that there was something foreign about these things; it was that these things did not belong to us. This sun had never come to our city. It was not Oakland's star.

The next day the district cancelled classes again, and said this time they did not know when school would start up. That morning, as if by prearranged signal, we cleared our classrooms. Those of us who had children paid them a few dollars to help with the heavy lifting; the rest of us labored alone, unpeeling carefully taped posters and art projects, wiping stray ink from the whiteboards, packing pamphlets and textbooks into cardboard boxes that we piled in front of the gates and carried one by one to the trunks of our cars. Our children crawled under desks and unstuck cracked old gum from their metal undersides, laughing through the small blue masks we had fit over their faces. Somewhere in the midst of this cleaning one of us found a few others in the teachers' lounge, and said what each of us had already known: she had called her grown-up daughter, who lived in New York, and there had been no answer. No answer from her brother in Boston or her parents in Los Angeles. The television had ceased to broadcast national news, statewide news, reality shows, soap operas; even the radio carried no voices. There was only the quiet whispering of the ash.

We appeared to each other in the courtyard like ghosts, silhouettes bursting into color and then fading again. We carried each other's detritus and swept each other's classroom floors. When we were done, a little before noon, we gathered by the gates, and clasped each other's hands, and kissed each other on the cheek, lips touching thin blue cloth touching skin. We told each other how very good it had been to work together. Then we let go, and went to our cars, and rolled up the windows, and listened to the low cough of our own engines.

At home, around half past one, I startled: I had forgotten my favorite book at school. I said this to my husband, though I did not know if he was listening, and I tied my mask back onto my face. Then I drove up through and through the greyness, past the BART station and the cemetery, into the winding hills. The streets were empty; I did not even have to use the teachers' parking lot. I unlocked the gates and walked down across the lawn, around the library, and into the building which housed the classroom where I had once taught.

My book was on my desk, just where I had left it. I picked it up, went into the hall, pulled my keys from my purse and locked the door of my classroom behind me.

When I heard my key click, I heard another noise, coming from the classroom next to mine. It was a soft sound; if I hadn't been listening for the lock, I would never have heard it. It was not a sound of breathing or speaking. It was a soft rustling, like dry leaves. I took a step to the right and put my hand to that classroom's doorknob—it was not locked—and eased it open, and put my eye to the crack.

They were there, all of them, every child whose parents had taken them away to the safety of the mountains. Each of them sitting at attention, with their faces faded as old newspaper. None of them were wearing masks. At the front of the classroom was the woman who had gone into San Francisco, and she was speaking, or trying to speak; her mouth was moving, but she was making no sound.

I opened the door just a little further. None of them moved.

I pushed it fully open and walked into the classroom. None of their heads turned. I said the name of one of the students; he did not look at me. I reached out to my fellow teacher and touched her hand, and I watched as her body shuddered and swirled and fell in clouds of soft fine greyness to the carpet below.

They stood, then, the Oaklanders who had reached the mountains, the Oaklanders who had escaped the smoke, the Oaklanders who had left our city for the higher ground without looking back. They stood and they pressed towards me, reaching out their hands, drifting through the desks and the chairs, and when they touched me they burst into grey, three of them at a time, five, ten, and I began to cough, and could not stop coughing. They would not stop coming. They would not stop dissolving, and yet they would not stop coming. I felt buried, buried under them, under their ash and their silence and their unceasing, limitless want. I felt like the city, vanished into endless softness. I felt like the sun.

Emery Robin is an Oakland-born and New York-based writer, previously published on *Tor.com* and in *Spark: A Creative Anthology*. When not busy reading, Emery is interested in propaganda, marginalia, and rock 'n' roll, and can be found on Twitter at @emwrobin.

When the Haze Descends

Shikhandin

When the haze descends
upon this sun-speared land, already wet
with sweat and tropical rain, clouds are veiled,
and there is smoke
in the air. Everything is a dismal grey.

Beneath September's scented moon
the flames of lanterns link
together like lovers' hands. Ghosts
let loose for a day, rise
to meet the haze.

My heart turns wistful. Longing
for things I had once abhorred—the acrid blue
of spent crackers. The noise. The oil
of lamps defying a moon
mourning for the night.

I sniff around for autumn's nip
right here in scoops of briny air.
My children are oblivious of my pain,
my friends aghast at my embrace
of the haze.

This polluting dust and smoke,
poverty's export, falling
like toxic pollen on their children—
that's their haze.

I walk under open skies tiara'd by
Singapore's cityscape, and the static
of this wired metropolis hisses. I
walk on to meet the chins of street lamps
growing fuzzy beards of light.

The smell of insects roasting
in the dying embers
of spent fireworks. A dusk
hanging low in the sky. And a strange
wind murmuring, as if to itself,
a soliloquy about a land
that gropes in the sea for rock and sand.

Note: Around September each year, fires from vegetation burning in Indonesia affect Singapore's air.

Shikhandin is the nom de plume of an Indian writer who writes for adults and children. She is an alumnus of The Anam Cara Writing Workshop, Ireland. Her published books, as Shikhandin, include *Immoderate Men* (Speaking Tiger), and *Vibhuti Cat* (Duckbill-Penguin-RHI). Contributor to *Magic Stories for Eight Year Olds* by Penguin RHI, and *Flipped: An Anthology of School and Sports Stories* by Harper Collins. A novel and a short story collection were published prior to her becoming Shikhandin. Her sci-fi story "Communal" was published simultaneously in two anthologies, *A Dying Planet* from Flametree Press and *Avatar* from Future Fiction in January 2020. Shikhandin's honours include: pushcart nominee by Aeolian Harp (USA) 2019, winner 2017 Children First Contest curated by Duckbill in association with Parag an initiative of Tata Trust, first prize Brilliant Flash Fiction Contest 2019 (USA), runner up Half and One Short Story Competition (India), Shortlist Erbacce Poetry Prize (UK), 35th Moon Prize (Writing in a Woman's Voice: USA), first runner up The DNA-OoP Short Story Contest 2016 (India), second Prize India Currents Katha Short Story Contest 2016 (USA), first prize Anam Cara Short Fiction Competition 2012 (Ireland), long list Bridport Poetry Prize 2006 (UK), finalist Aesthetica Poetry Contest 2010 (UK), Pushcart nominee by Cha: An Asian Literary Journal 2011 (Hong Kong). Shikhandin's poetry and prose have been published worldwide.

Everything that Happens

William Squirrell

Robot Cities roam the baking deserts of the ocean beds like Baba Yaga huts. They strut about on titanic rusting legs so tall that to fall from the crotch to the ground takes a human 30 seconds. They sing songs, these Robot Cities, melancholic folk songs with introspective lyrics. They sing about shame and adoration, they sing about that sweet moment when love has found you out but your lover has not, they sing about becoming and not-becoming.

Humans infest them like lice. They forage on the cracked carapaces for petrel eggs, hunting wadi monkeys, scavenging for spare parts. They sing along with the cities as they work, as the cities stride about, they lose themselves in the words. They lose themselves under the searing white skies, enjoying the breeze and the infinite views, enjoying the beautiful music.

In the long evenings the Robot Cities squat on the precipitous decline of continental shelves, plucking the parasites from one another. They clean itching skin with gigantic, marvelously dexterous toes, catching between tungsten carbide digits the monkeys and the humans that lingered too long. Catching them and popping them.

"Everything that happens to me," the Robot Cities sing, "has happened to someone else too."

"Everything that happens to me," they sing, "will one day happen to you."

Much safer in the tangled interior, in the avenues and the streets through which the twisting wind creeps, the humans hide their children in shadowy places like spider eggs. They tap water from the pipes that cool the creaking reactors. The stolen moisture collects in them, in the humans, in their livers and their kidneys, in their blood, radioactive, congealing, concentrating into lumps and bumps and tumors, into the braille of survival.

"What do we do if it dies?" a child asks.

"If what dies?"

"Our Mamapapa."

"The Mamapapas never die."

The humans tell their children stories of how the Mamapapas once slept on the ground. They were reclining cities. But the humans proliferated to such a degree that their activities inflamed the skins of the cities and the cities woke. The cities stood up and became the Mamapapas.

They tell their children how the world used to be covered with water but the Mamapapas drank it all. The Mamapapas are cursed with thirst. They wander the desert searching for something to drink.

They tell their children visitors used to come from the other Mamapapas. They tell their children how the visitors climbed up and down the legs. How they traversed the wretched ocean floor, picking their way through the bones of the birds and the monkeys and the humans that littered the ground. They tell the children how the visitors brought a plague, a virus that killed thousands. How they shoveled the bodies out of the Mamapapas. Tens of thousands. The bodies fell through the air like rain and settled on the earth like dust.

The humans sing to their children: "Everything that happens to me, has happened to someone else too. Everything that happens to me, will one day happen to you."

They teach their children to give thanks to their Mamapapa for food, shelter, and water. They teach them to love their Mamapapa. They teach their children to fear their Mamapapa.

The Mamapapas roam the baking beds of the ocean on their colossal backward-kneed legs. They sing songs to each other about the great ring of the horizon. About the arbitrariness of existence. They sing songs about incalculable loss. And humans infest them like lice.

William Squirrell is a Canadian living in western Pennsylvania. His work has appeared in *Flapperhouse*, *Monkeybicycle*, *Sundog Lit*, *decomP magazinE*, and other publications. He is the editor of www.bigecho.org. More information can be found at www.blindsquirrell.com and on twitter @billsquirrell.

POUR FAIRE
LA DIFFÉRENCE,
METTONS FIN
À L'INDIFFÉRENCE

lady meet mr robinson

Don Dussault

momma yell from the kitchen julius buzz her in.

buzz who

my ol high school chum dont you forget turn the hall light on

hall light dont work momma

hall black like the devils ass you open the parlor door get light down there

i done it momma

she call it a parlor goodwill couch goodwill chairs i hear this come up the steps high heels who wear them things

mr robinson watch at the door lady look scared i say he gentle wont hurt you none

lady wear cool clothes nice coat swag me out and she got big smile for me i say i am julius

i am seven keisha is five we sit quiet on the couch lady say please to meet you

mr robinson sniff lady she look fussed till he settle down by the door

momma bring in tea momma ask we wants tea or water no thank you momma

momma and lady talk been long time they got married divorced while lady cant help her self she sneak peeks at mr robinson she see he clean sleek long fur big strong dog

mr robinson he lay by the door thinkin what dogs think

lady and momma they do talk lots and us kids sit quiet to show we got good manners us listen we dont get visits much lady got plenty bones from city cause second husband killed on subway job momma pour more tea lady ask me why dog name mr robinson

i say grandpa seen jackie robinson in ebbets field long time ago i seen him on gray telvisin grandpa he gone now

lady watch mr robinson she think it funny us in east harlem sooty rooms on snap and welfare we got this big fancy dog he eat like we is rich folks she think we put on like we got dog show dog she dont say so police siren go by fast be dark soon lady say she treat us to supper wheres a fine restraunt round here

i seen this place family up from new orlins they cook jambelia we never had none

we goin out the door mr robinson get up momma say they dont let dogs in restraunts

i say mr robinson you got to sit and stay

lady say fine handsome dog you takes good care of him

keisha say we dig brush him

lady say you likes a big dog

i say we need a big dog he keep the rats out

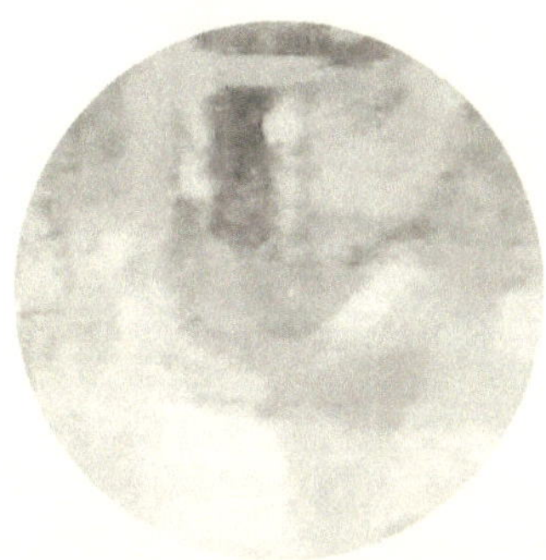

Don lives in the San Francisco Bay Area. His history includes a MA in English literature and postgrad study in linguistics. He's published poetry, fiction and nonfiction in several literary publications. So far, excerpts from four fictions, among other stuff, appear on his website under construction, https://dondussault.net/

Great Auk

Pinguinus impennis

Holly Hughes

Once, flocks of great auks nested on the rocks
off the coast of the North Atlantic. The first bird

to be called a penguin, they were built to swim,
but slow, defenseless on land. Pairs mated for life,

nesting shoulder to shoulder in dense rookeries,
laying one egg on bare rock, taking turns tending

the egg until it hatched. Devoted parents, they cared
for their young even after they'd fledged;

adults were seen swimming, chicks perched
on their backs. In those days, a sighting of great auks

quickened a sailor's heart, signaled landfall ahead.
Their end came when the Europeans' love for featherbeds

brought hunters in search of down (after every eider
had been plucked, gone). To loosen their plumage,

auks were boiled in cauldrons over fires fed with the oil
of auks killed before them, since there was little wood to be found.

In 1830, a volcano erupted off the tip of Iceland, submerging
the last nesting colony on *Geirfuglasker,* great auk rock.

Refugees, the auks moved to the island of Eldey. There,
on July 3, 1844, the last pair was killed by hunters

gathering specimens for a museum. Here's how one hunter
described the scene: *I took him by the neck and he flapped his wings.*

He made no cry. I strangled him.

Note: Great auk specialist John Wolley interviewed the two men who killed the last birds, and Sigurour Ísleifsson described the act; the words in italics are his.

Holly J. Hughes' chapbook *Passings* received an American Book Award in 2017; in 2019, four poems were set to music by composer Edie Hill and performed by The Crossings choir in Philadelphia and New York City. She's also the author of *Hold Fast*, *Sailing by Ravens*, and coauthor of *The Pen and The Bell: Mindful Writing in a Busy World*. She's a graduate of Pacific Lutheran University's low-residency MFA program, where she served on the staff for 12 years. Currently, she leads writing and mindfulness workshops in the northwest and consults as a writing coach. She can be reached at hollyjhughes.com.

"Great Auk" originally appeared in *Passings*, first published by Expedition Press in 2016 and reprinted by Wandering Aengus Press in 2019.

A Rare Hybrid of Dung Beetle and Lion

Noa Covo

The only television shows I cannot bear to watch are nature documentaries. I see them and am reminded that the animals in the titular roles are dying, will be dead before I get to travel and behold them. Their Latin names spoken in gravelly voices are almost obituaries by now.

"There goes *Panthera leo*, stalking its prey. Too bad it'll be gone by 2050." The narrator seems to say: "Such a wonderful beast that you've never seen and never will! Won't you miss it?"

Of course, the sad thing is, I will miss it. I'll probably even cry over the damn thing. Every time an exotic creature takes its last breath, I find myself wishing I was at its deathbed. The day I heard six vultures were poisoned to death just a few hours north of me, making them almost certainly extinct under my country's skies, I thought of the lions that used to walk the soil under my feet, soil turned to concrete. As a child, when I heard that lions used to wander not so far from my house, I was filled with wonder. Now, I think of how I'll tell my children there used to be vultures here, too.

There is nature in the city I call home, hidden in between crushed soda cans and drifting plastic wrappers. The river that used to be a liquid graveyard is slowly healing. There are the sparrows and the wagtails, birds to which songs are dedicated, patchworks of what came before the city. One could say: they are the protectors, they were here first, we love them for it. Opposing them is a long, decorous line of creatures, living litter, dropped just as carelessly as soda cans, and equally appreciated. The jellyfish invade the beach once a summer. They aren't supposed to be there, but nobody told them the Suez Canal is for human use only. The bright green parakeets that fill the skies escaped from the zoo. The angry-eyed mynas that fight them for territory did as well. It isn't their fault they're here, and that the vultures up north are nearly gone, but it's hardly a fair trade.

Walking the city, I look up between the buildings that act as shutters between me and the sky and curse every bright green flash I see. Only now does it occur to me that we may be under custody as much as the parakeets were. The city around me is a quarantine. *Homo sapiens* in, wildlife out. We keep it so, with poisoned corpses left for birds of prey and tawny skins stretched out for our rugs. If we leak out of the city, as we are prone to do, we will ruin what is around us just as the parakeets and mynas slashed apart the biological web of the recovering river. The invaders flock around us. After all, we brought them here, into the concrete jungle.

I imagine that I want to live in the country, amongst the pristine nature, without our new addendums, or at least, with fewer of them. But then I think of the felled trees for my home and the split habitats for my roads and consign myself to the unforgiving concrete and the towering buildings. We humans deserve being confined in our urban prisons, but that doesn't mean I don't spend my days dreaming of escape, dreaming of being not quite human.

I like to imagine myself the subject of a nature documentary, with a grim narrator reporting my plight. Perhaps overpopulation will kill me; maybe climate change will destroy my home. Maybe a photograph of my suffering will win someone a prestigious prize. Maybe there will be a fund in my honor, a picture of my genus on a popular website.

I try not to kid myself. I am not a rare bird or lion. I am not royalty. I don't have the heart of a *Panthera leo*, like a certain King of England. I do not fly a crest of arms emblazoned with a vulture. I am far from being the last of a genetic line. I am no Salome, last independent ruler of Judea and last female leopard in that same desert, queens of dwindling hope. If I were an animal, I wouldn't be shown struggling in the jaws of a polar bear or torn open by a gunshot. I'm not an unwelcome newcomer, either, not a bright green parakeet or angry myna, roosting in places I shouldn't be. If I were an animal, I would be a dung beetle, strolling along under a scorching sun, uninhibited by the falling birthrate of lions.

After deciding this, I was informed, although not on a nature documentary, that the dung beetle rolls its crap in a line of cosmic significance, following the Milky Way. A dung beetle must roll his ball of dung away from the rest of the dung beetles, in a straight line. He cannot falter, or he risks the ball being stolen by others, and he, a creature smaller than the palm of my hand, can see starlight that

I cannot begin to grasp, and he follows it. Perhaps this should not surprise me, for he was once an Egyptian god, rolling the sun across the sky. That was when he was a scarab, incarnate of the sun god Ra, but Ra has long faded away from most of us, and what is left is a dung-rolling creature, travelling through insignificant wastelands. Scarab and lion used to be king and protector. Mighty Sekhmet the lion goddess, guarding the dung beetle's slow walk across the heavens. She was so powerful her breath created the desert.

The two have separated since the ancient Egyptians. Lions on every coat of arms, in every tale, while their king is burrowed into the obscurity of the desert, and perhaps it is in the best interest of the latter. Richard the Lionheart came to the Holy Land when lions still lived near my apartment, but they left when he did, hunted by the Crusaders. The lions that now roam the desert, the same desert Sekhmet formed with a single breath, are scarce; they no longer have to protect Ra, but rather themselves. I wonder if the dung beetles would be on endangered watch lists if their glory continued after Ra, if killing them was a conquest. Maybe I would be watching them on a nature show as they rolled one last ball in a heavenly line.

Once, as I deplored the state of the world, I thought myself far more puny than majestic. The city can do that to you, but even the mass of buildings doesn't compare with the news piling up around me. The streets I walk are nothing compared to the data I scroll through each day, weather reports, knowledge crowding up like cars in traffic. The sheer information about nature used to dwarf me. Every percentage about the climate, every new disappearing species, every sign I held and every lecture I listened to hammered in my insignificance. I became sure I was a dung beetle, with only the power to push my own dung as the few lions that walk among us burned my future.

I didn't know where those lions—oil giants, company owners, billionaires—lived, but I often assumed they must be far out in the country, away from the skyscrapers hemming the rest of us in. I thought that perhaps they did not understand, these predators, what they were doing. One of the stories about Sekhmet tells of her going into a blood frenzy, destroying all in her path. She was calmed only by Ra tricking her into drinking red beer, sending her into a drunken stupor. I did not think anyone was capable of subduing our lions, our world leaders, and was certain we were failed dung beetles, merely insects and not kings. Bloody report after bloody report, I wished the world could fall asleep so we could start afresh.

Only lately, walking down cracked sidewalks, pushing my own ball of shit in front of me, have I started to realize how much bigger I am compared to a dung beetle, and how much smaller compared to a lion, and started to consider that perhaps I am a combination of both. As I read reports about trees being planted, plastics being banned, schools striking, I no longer feel so small. A teenager may be a dung beetle, but a group of them is something entirely different, something that has grown a pair of claws. Dung beetles know to follow the stars, the scarab used to be king, after all, but the lion is the fighter—and fighting we are. My generation, and others, fighting for the vultures and the lions and most importantly, ourselves, and I fight along with them, part lion, part dung beetle.

My inner nature show narrator, studying the hybrid I've realized is me, is at peace as he babbles on about eventual extinction. I'm a specimen approaching endangered status, apparently, but I've also rolled a ball of shit across the desert, no simple feat. I push my ball of thoughts in front of me as I stalk fallen pieces of litter. I realize there is a strange sort of balance inside me. I am aware of climate change, of ecological breakdown. I know the ramifications: the heat, the cold, that we will have to adapt to later if we don't change now. But I also choose to hope that no matter the damage we do to our planet, it too will adapt. There will always be life: the jellyfish, the parakeets, the dung beetles. We are murderers, we have killed vultures, lions, but we have invited in the bloodthirsty mynas. The mynas will ruin the current order and create a new one, one in which we, along with many others, may be left behind. It would serve us right. If we, *Homo sapiens,* had a nature narrator, he would be speaking of the long period we must prepare for. "They can save themselves," he would say urgently. "But they are too foolish to do so." Then he would continue to talk about all the other wonderful animals, adapting, evolving, in ways it would be wise for us to do too, as humankind carries on hunting stars.

My imaginary hybrid self, the beetle lion, has come to the conclusion that living things will always remain, even if they're an awkward sort of compromise between an Egyptian god and the king of the savannah, or a quickly disappearing species and a dung beetle. It's true that the vultures up north are nearly gone, that the parakeets are biological invaders, the ecological system as we know it is falling apart. It's true I may never get to see a lion in person, definitely not anywhere near my house, but the jellyfish will keep coming to hunt my bare legs instead. Our world is falling apart, but maybe we'll be able to put it together again.

Despite my newfound hope, of myself and of our planet, I still cannot bear to watch nature documentaries, but when I walk down the street in the shade of the skyscrapers, I know I too have a path of cosmic significance, a fair shot at survival.

Despite both these things, I've already started to miss the lions.

Noa Covo is an aspiring teenage writer and Fridays For Future activist. Her work has been published in *Museum Anthology*, a Didcot Writers anthology, and *5x5*, a literary magazine. She can be found on Twitter @covo_noa.

Alive Between the Bands

Laurinda Lind

In a twenty-year temperature inversion
California walks in to me through
the windows of a hot car with no
air conditioning, it's summer and
the heater is full-blast, it's a hundred-
degree day, I am younger and California
is cleaner, the engine doesn't self-

eject and it jets out oil all across
the country. This awful air of
ourselves, we have nowhere to drive

but down into it, the freeway
folding over and under, everything
settling which also means seething,
the old rocks with all the time
in-between them and the road

only a ribbon of exhaust
held harmless between the jaws
of a geologic age.

Your Second Shift After the Factory

Laurinda Lind

Once the doors shut behind you,
shift to saving yourself.
Try steam and chest percussions
to chase factory smoke out of
your lungs, you need to be a human
still. Which is hard to do with dioxin,
so get that out too, with ghee.
If it goes as far
as your liver

then a long shot is to blast
it by eating dandelion buds.
Also asbestos comes in like
a cloud of unseeable needles
and won't like to leave but
while you are learning how long
you have left to live and they are pulling
the professional

smile down over their lips
at the clinic, look up
hydrogen peroxide
and hum that to yourself
along with vitamin C

until you can find a doctor
who doesn't want you dead.
Oh, and Atlantic dulse,
a seaweed that strips out mercury, so
you can start filling up with it
all over again in the morning.

Laurinda Lind lives in New York's North Country. Some publications/ acceptances are in *Blue Earth Review*, *Comstock Review*, *Midwest Quarterly*, *Paterson Literary Review*, and *Spillway*; also anthologies *Visiting Bob: Poems Inspired by the Life and Work of Bob Dylan* (New Rivers Press) and *AFTERMATH: Explorations of Loss and Grief* (Radix Media). In 2018, she won first place in both the Keats-Shelley Prize for adult poetry and the New York State Fair poetry competition.

PORTE PLACE D'ITALIE

Billy Ray's Small Appliance Rehabilitation

Geoffrey W. Cole

The community's gardener, Mr. Ussander, tosses the clock radio on the counter and demands a refund. The radio looks holy to me. He tells me to plug it in. "It is Well With My Soul" belts out of the mono speaker and the clock glows the unmistakable blue of an LED.

"My wife wants to know why you are so intent on condemning us to eternal damnation."

He won't touch the thing, despite my assurances that we will finish the rehabilitation, so I count out the bills of his refund. He crosses the street, back to Revelation, the only Grahamite community in Toronto. Once the customer leaves, I slip into the workshop. David's legs stick out from beneath a big wood-panelled hi-fi cabinet.

"That's the third refund this week," I say. He's been working on the cabinet for days now, way longer than it should take to replace the digital amplifier. I count backward to the last time I filled his prescription, and I swear. "This is more than just a hi-fi rehabilitation, isn't it?"

David slides out from beneath the cabinet, the sleeves of his Oxford rolled up. Purple blotches cover the exposed flesh. "I've made a great discovery, Billy Ray. This time it will be different."

I slam the clock radio down on the workbench. The last time he tried to build a time machine, he almost burned down the shop. "The therapist warned against this kind of behaviour. The past only exists in your mind. You can't go back there. You can't fix it."

"The Lord rewards patience."

"I reward you for rehabilitating appliances, and you're doing a shit job of it."

I go back to my perch behind the counter. He can never go back there, but I can. I slip the Backflasher out from beneath the counter and press the cerephones to my forehead. I go looking for something, anything, that can save him. And I go back because that night is the night he took his first step out of their world and into mine.

I open my favorites and go back to that night fifteen years ago when David discovered his Shift.

Tuesday evening, the second to last week of Grade Ten. I wade through the filthy waters of Highland Creek. Diapers, tires, broken bottles, circuit boards, and the occasional bloated animal carcass line the bank. The creek flows toward a red brick wall, and at the spot the oil-slicked liquid flows through the culvert, I hold my breath, duck, and swim a short length of darkness.

David meets me in Revelation. I come out dripping and itchy and he rushes me along the bank of the reservoir full of discoloured water, past the water treatment plant his father built, to the plant's outlet where the creek spills out clear and pure in the summer evening light. I wash off the industrial sewage and we go looking for the girls.

Two piles of clothing sit on the banks of Baptismal Pool Number Three. The girls call to us from the water. Anja and Rebecca. One for each of us, even though I am no more interested in Anja than she is in me. They bob in the middle of the pool, the white promise of their breasts hidden just below the surface. We duck under one of the weeping willows that line the creek and undress. The chastity vow I made when I joined David's high school burns in my ears as I watch him peel off his uniform.

Warm slices of sunset dance across David's hairless chest. I pretend my erection is for the girls. In that partitioned sunlight, I can't be sure about the three purple spots I notice just below David's left shoulder blade. I brush them with the tips of my fingers, the spots warm and sweat-damp. We find two more in a cluster on his right thigh. David recoils at the sight of them.

"They can't be Bernie Blotches," he says. He wets his thumb and tries to rub them off.

"What's taking so long?" Rebecca says.

"The water's divine," Anja says.

David slides his shirt back on and buttons it up. "I can't let her see this." He trembles beneath the willow branches, shoes in his hand. "Please, Billy Ray. We have to go."

"You owe me one skinny dip," I say as I dress.

We steal the girls' clothes. The two of them scream as we run down the bank. We leave their clothes on the picnic table by Baptismal Pool Number Four. David doesn't want to go home; he can't face his mother yet. I think he's already decided she was the transgressor. So we call from the pay phone at the gas station. David's father, Adam Mercer—or who he assumed until that night was his father—answers. David tells him that we are sleeping over at Robert O'Leary's house, the first lie I've ever heard him tell his parents. I pick up my phone and glasses from the lock box. The booze-soaked guard at Revelation's east gate doesn't notice us duck past.

Outside the gates, a steady stream of cars, buses, and streetcars crawl by along the eight-lanes of Lawrence Avenue. David watches it all in wide-eyed apprehension. He's never been out of the compound without a chaperone before.

We take the streetcar three stops, then transfer to a bus. A Brawny Baby is strapped into a wheelchair up at the front, her sitter immersed in a VR headset beside her. I try to pull David past the Brawny, but he stops at her side. She looks like a botched attempt at cloning a gorilla. Thick coils of muscle protrude from her triple-XL T-shirt and drool leaks past her bite guard. Every bare patch of flesh is marked by the same purple blotches I found on David's white skin. David kneels beside her as the bus rolls away from the curb and places his hands on her massive forearm.

"The Lord still loves you," he says.

She spits out her bite guard. Great dark eyes focus on David. She knocks him to the ground and shouts: "Drink."

The sitter strips off her VR rig and crams a two-litre bottle of Enervade into the Brawny Baby's sucking mouth.

"That's assault," the sitter says. "See if I don't put in a claim for workplace stress and discomfort. Slip me two grand, I might change my mind."

David reaches for his wallet.

"Make that claim," I say. "And I'll tell your employer you were jacked in when you were supposed to be sitting."

"Drink," the giant roars. She throws the empty bottle to

ground. "Drink!"

The sitter searches her bag for another bottle. We hide at the back of the bus.

"You can't go around touching people," I say.

"That will be me. A giant strapped to a chair."

"We don't even know what kind of Baby you are. Most rational explanation is that your real dad was a Beautiful Baby who charmed her pants off."

I don't mean to say it, but I know he is thinking the same thing.

"The whore," he says.

The next stop is mine. Mom is working the late shift at the restaurant so we have the place to ourselves. I try to get him to eat, but everything in the fridge is GMO'd or manufactured offshore. Eventually I find some dried apples from a Grahamite community in Cobourg we visited on a school trip last October.

"She witnessed for a year on the West Coast during her first Mission," he says, jaw grinding the leathery strips of apple. "Met Dad out there and came back pregnant. Fooled him ever since."

"We should talk to Pastor Kline tomorrow. He'll know what to do."

"'Come ye out from among them and be ye separate'. I know exactly what has to be done."

David stuffs another piece of near-fossilized apple into his mouth. As I watch, a cluster of Bernie Blotches blossom on his cheek, the bruise from an ancient wound his body only now remembers.

The door to the shop chimes. I pop off the cerephones and slide the Backflasher into a drawer: Grahamites don't like to see their service providers using forbidden tech. Into the fading memory of that summer night walks a gorgeous Grahamite woman, blonde hair sprayed into a golden mass on top of her head. She peels off thin leather driving gloves as she approaches the counter.

"That your Fairlane parked out front?" I say. She nods. "They don't make them like they used to."

"I understand you do make them like they used to," she says.

Her voice has that breathy quality leading ladies adopted in movies from the 1950s.

"Appliances, sure. Not automobiles."

"It's an automobile I'm after," she says. "A '57 Bel Air, to be precise. I'm told you're honest, and that you do good work."

I straighten up. Working on a car would be good for David. It could mean weeks of work. Maybe even enough to knock him out of this Fascination.

"None better in the province, when it comes to appliances. For automobiles, we usually ship from California or Cuba, but in special circumstances, we've been known to do the work in-house. What do you have in mind?"

She places her gloves on the counter and makes a show of looking at the clocks, power tools, toasters, and other appliances in my cabinet. Sweat rolls in small droplets to the low neck of her dress.

"It's my twentieth wedding anniversary. I found the '57 in Etobicoke. Thoroughly desecrated, of course, but once you make it pure, my husband will love it."

"Won't be cheap to fix a car like that," I say. The refunds of the past week have taken a deep cut of our revenue and I have to make up the rent somehow.

She shrugs. "My husband tells me I needn't worry about money. Name your price, I'm sure it will be fair."

"I'll have to see the car first."

She writes down the address of the wrecker on the back of her husband's card. She is Mrs. Robert Thrangle, from the Grahamite community in Kemptville, outside Ottawa. Long drive in one of those old cars. I promise to call with the quote. After the Fairlane chugs off, I walk back to the workshop.

David is soldering a vacuum tube into an electrical board. In the time since I last came in, he's attached two chairs to the old hi-fi cabinet, abandoning all pretence that this is a standard rehabilitation. The LED-blighted clock radio sits forgotten on the workbench.

I tell him about the Bel Air. He keeps working. I tell him it will be enough money to cover rent for a couple months. He finishes the connection and places the soldering iron on the workbench.

"Might even be enough to pay for another prescription."

He looks up from behind the electrical board.

"Those pills are nothing but shackles to confine my intellect.

I won't take them again."

"Will you at least come with me to look at the car? They are airing game four of the '59 World Series tomorrow. We could listen on the way back."

"I'll listen to it here."

He picks up another vacuum tube and solders it in place.

It`s too late in the day to start the journey—the highway isn't safe after dark—so I pack a few things and plan to leave in the morning.

David won't come upstairs for dinner. I bring the soup down to him, and when I check before bed, it has congealed untouched beside the clock radio. During his previous Fascination, he only stopped eating at the very end. He might not want to take his drugs, but I'll be damned if I will let this go any further. There is a pharmacy near the wreckers, and it is far enough away that they won't recognize me there. I get out the Backflasher.

A cold Friday afternoon, two years ago, right at the end of his previous Fascination. David struggles to walk as we stumble toward the gates of Lakeshore Hospital.

"The machine will send me back," he says as he struggles against me. "Let me keep working."

Snow hisses underfoot. He weighs less than sixty kilos. I drag him through the gate like he is a sullen child. At the entrance to the main building, a man standing above a pile of rags shouts as we approach.

"Hear ye, hear ye, a pair of deuces and a pound of pudding. Step right up, young men, to this, the greatest show this side of the pond. Gift horses for all, mouths unexamined, we guarantee. No fillings, no funerals. Just good fun for the little ones."

He wears a long overcoat and wool top hat. Above the thick scarf wrapped around his neck, his face is covered in purple blotches.

"I need help," I say. "Can you fetch a doctor?"

"Don't interrupt," the pile of rags says. A woman is entombed within, her bare, blotchy hands trembling in the cold, yet still managing to write in a thick notebook.

"Interruptions are intolerable," the man in the top hat says. "But how's this for tolerance? No refunds!"

The woman in the rags writes down everything the top hat Baby says. She underlines words, circles others, and connects circled words to one another with thick black lines.

"Don't lock me up in here, Billy Ray," David says. "These people are sick. Let me finish my work."

Dr. LaRose meets with us after I pay her five-hundred-dollar consultation fee. Five minutes of inspecting David later, and she tells me he is suffering a Fascination, a psychological break Brainy Babies often exhibit post-Shift. Googling has told me much the same. From the history I give her, she figures this is his fifth Fascination. The original Bernard's Brainy Baby Serum was designed to stimulate neural development in children and create hyper-intelligent youth. At puberty, when the Shift hits, that neural development continues, old synapses restart and new ones develop, they short-circuit and invaginate, leading to the sort of repetitive, obsessive behaviour I was seeing in David.

"What can we do about it?" I say.

She writes out a prescription and hands it to me. I don't take it. "Do you have anything simpler? He was a Grahamite."

"We don't look too fondly on electroshock therapy here." She places the prescription back on her desk. "Why didn't you bring him in earlier?"

"I could handle it."

"We can handle it better," she says. She slides a pamphlet across the table. "Thanks to the class-action settlement, once the patients are committed, you won't have to pay a thing. We can book him today."

"He's second generation."

Dr. LaRose leans back in her chair.

"A Grahamite who is also a second-generation Bernard Baby?"

"He was a Grahamite, until the Shift."

"That must have been ugly. In any case, if he's second generation, he wasn't part of the class action. He can stay here, but it will be quite expensive."

I ask for the prescription. When she hands it to me, I pause the Backflasher and forge a copy complete with the good doctor's signature. Then I go back to the memory.

The nurse at the front desk sells me the pills. I make her help me hold David down to get him to swallow the forbidden technology. A little while later, he gets drowsy. The two Babies are still outside when we leave, the Brainy woman in rags chattering as she scribbles in her notebook. The Boisterous man in the top-hat shouts: "Come back soon, y'all. There's so much left to see and do and you don't want to miss a wink."

As we wait for the streetcar, snow begins to fall. David leans against me, his body so thin beneath the layers I wrapped him in. I hold him while he snores and I look up into the falling snow and for the first time since he stopped eating I can breathe again.

Metal clatters in the workshop downstairs. David mutters a polite curse. I shut down the Backflasher and hold onto that moment at the end of his last Fascination, David in my arms, the cold air in my lungs. He so rarely lets me touch him. I let the memory lull me to sleep.

In the morning, I bring David toast and poached eggs from the only market left in Revelation, but he ignores me as I set it down on the workbench. At five-thirty, I check out a community car. All twenty-eight lanes on the 401 are full by the time I make it onto the highway. My autodriver does its best to find a lane, but so does everyone else's.

Three hours later, I arrive in Etobicoke. The address Mrs. Robert Thrangle gave me was for a wrecker not far off the highway. I find the car at the back of the lot, the front end crumpled, that chrome maw deformed. Still, it is a beauty. The pinnacle of American automotive design. With that vehicle stretched out in front of me, I can understand why Grahamites consider the years between 1954 and 1965 to be the most holy in history, and why they choose to live like Americans of that era.

The car's previous owner made a suite of modern improvements—auto-driver, climate control, HUD, immersion sound, electric drive—and they will all have to be stripped out and replaced with the sacred technology of the era before it will be ready for Mrs.

Robert Thrangle. Just what David needs. The wrecker says he could get me the car later that day if I want.

I put the quote together on the way to the pharmacy. Over the telephone, Mrs. Robert Thrangle tells me the price sounds fair and offers to wire me an advance. Kind people, Grahamites. I thank her and put a call in to the wrecker just as the car pulls up to the pharmacy.

The woman behind the counter doesn't take a second look at my forged prescription; she just doles out the pills and gives me the bill. The drugs are expensive, almost a month's rent for a month's supply, but with the cash from the Bel Air rehabilitation, we can afford it.

The car predicts another four hours to get home, so I take out the Backflasher and go back to the night David spent at my apartment, our first night together, as the two of us tried to figure out what kind of Bernie Baby had fathered him.

David does push-ups and squats until his muscles give out. I record how many he does and compare the results to the number he did an hour earlier. There is no improvement. It doesn't look like his real father was a Brawny Baby. At least he won't end up like the woman on the bus. He goes online, a rare transgression of Grahamite orthodoxy, and answers three different IQ tests. He's always been bright, but he isn't getting any brighter. The results rule out a Brainy Baby as a father. Though I think his spots are darling, he hasn't gotten any cuter since the start of his Shift, and he was never really considered a good looking guy by the girls at school, other than Rebecca, which means he probably isn't a Beautiful Baby either.

"Maybe they aren't Bernie Blotches?" I say, trying to sound hopeful.

"The Shift happens at puberty," he says. "The traits are amplified and warped then. Mine are just coming in; maybe we can't detect them yet."

By that point in the night, we are both up on our research into Bernard's Syndrome. During the development of the drugs, each Serum tested so well on the children in the trials that the products were approved and put to market before the test batch of kids hit puberty. Hundreds of thousands of parents purchased Bernard's Baby Serums for their progeny. A whole generation of children was born Beautiful, Boisterous, Brainy, Brawny, and other adjectives that stretched marketing alliteration to its limit. As the kids from the first trials hit their early teens, their Shifts started, and they went spotty. Bernie Blotches appeared on Beautiful Babies as readily as they did on Boisterous kids, but the Blotches were the only trait they all shared. During the Shift, the traits that made them prodigies and child celebrities were amplified way out of proportion. Praxit Inc., who'd purchased the Serum from Bernard in the early days, divested itself of the product line and pulled the Serum from the shelves. The damage was already done. Those same hundreds of thousands of parents were forced to watch as their children went from prodigies to freaks. Dr. Bernard killed himself. Dozens of lawsuits joined forces to suck cash from Praxit's bleeding husk, a messy affair that took the better part of a decade. Only after the lawsuits were settled did anyone realize that Bernard's Syndrome was inheritable.

My mother comes home around two that night. Bleary-eyed and stinking of simgarettes, she pours herself a cup of coffee and collapses on the couch.

"Why are you two up so late?" she says.

"School project," I say.

She grabs my arm. Her halitosis makes me gag.

"This is what flunking out looks like, Billy Ray," she says. She gestures at her polyester restaurant uniform. "I'm not working three jobs so you can flunk out. Study hard."

She fades back into the couch.

David steps up in front of her.

"Can I tell you a joke?" he says. Mom nods a head that appears to weigh tonnes. "How did Delilah know Sampson's door would be open?" Her shrug works just as hard to raise her shoulders. "Because she cut his locks off."

She makes a sound that might be laughter and starts to snore.

"Guess I'm not a Boisterous Baby either," he says.

We dig up articles on the rarer versions of Bernard's Serum, like Belonging Babies and Blazing Babies and the other poorly marketed serums, and David tests himself against them as best he can.

He compiles all the results in one of my school notebooks and looks for any single trait that stands out from the pack.

"Something has to stick," he says.

Mom's alarm goes off and she pulls herself off the couch, finishes the cup of cold coffee, and gets ready for work. It's four-thirty. By five, she's gone, and I am making breakfast. David is doing push-ups again.

"We should get ready for school," I say.

He holds up a spotted arm. "They won't let me through the gate."

I dig out Mom's make-up kit and go to work. By the time I'm done, all of David's spots are concealed and I even paint some colour into his pale cheeks. He looks so beautiful I want to kiss him. We leave for school.

Sick crows fight cancer-ridden gulls over the contents of the apartment building's garbage container. We take the bus and streetcar through Toronto's crowded streets. The AC is broken on the streetcar, so I touch-up David's foundation when we get off outside the gates to the compound.

"Promise me you won't do anything stupid," I say.

"'And touch not the unclean thing,'" he quotes.

We wait until one of the water trucks stops at the gate. It's an old '37 Ford, the back uncovered, the truck laden with crates of glass water bottles ready to be refilled. We jump in the back and duck under a tarp. Selling bottled water was one of Adam Mercer's suggestions to help fund the water treatment facility he designed for the community. Water purified the old-fashioned way is a hit with the wealthy people still living in Toronto and bottled water sales are one of the two main economic engines for the community. The other is also one of Adam's innovations: the tuition outside students like me pay to attend John the Baptist Secondary School.

The school bell tolls. At an intersection, we hop off and run through town. Wives in aprons bring in the mail. Husbands lug leather briefcases to their gleaming Plymouths and Studebakers. At the end of our fifteen-minute run, we come to John the Baptist.

The community might have been established to save the souls of the Grahamites who call it home, but that school is my salvation. After the fifth beating at my old high school landed me in the emergency room, my mother got me into John the Baptist. She took the extra jobs to pay the tuition. Parents pay good money for their children to attend a school system with zero incidents of mass shootings, stabbings, or poisonings. Mom's hard labour lets those men drive their Studebakers, lets the women drink wine before ten in the morning, and it lets me sit beside David without fear of ever having a limb broken because of whom I love.

As we run toward John the Baptist with fear of expulsion whipping me on, I try to remember my vow of punctuality, but the words I had to speak on my first day of school—vows of obedience, chastity, punctuality, and charity—bleed together like a watercolour tossed into a lake. All I can remember is Kline's deep, sexy voice and his Old Spice aftershave. And, how after the vows, he walked me to my classroom and pointed me to an empty chair beside this cute, old-school nerdy boy whose nostrils flared so much when I took my seat that I worried I'd stepped in something on the way in.

"David," he said, and offered his dry hand for me to shake. "Is that Mothra?" He pointed at the giant moth stenciled onto the pencil case I'd placed on the desk. It was. He smiled, his teeth blazing white in their fluoridated glory, and in that moment I knew this school was a good place.

The thought of losing that place, and the only real friend I have in the world, leaves me trembling as we run up the steps of the old school. I swing the front door open and halt. David slams into me.

In the front entrance of the school, David's mother Linda-Jane Mercer stands with her husband Adam. Both look equal parts concerned and furious. Beside them, Revelation's spiritual and political leader, Pastor Kline, gazes at his wristwatch.

"I knew it," Linda-Jane says, looking up at Adam. "How often have I said that boy is a bad influence on our son?"

The car interrupts the memory to tell me we've arrived.

Concrete and steel towers rise above the red brick walls of Revelation. Cranes extruded new apartment blocks within the old footprint of the community. In the fifteen years since David was expelled, we've watched Revelation whither. Without water sales and tuition from outside students and the other innovations Adam brought to Revelation, revenues declined. The Grahamites within the walls sold off chunks of their land to pay for ever-increasing property taxes. Well-tended lawns became parking garages, the Brightwater was paved over, and John the Baptist Secondary School was sold off and turned into high-end condominiums.

Only a few hundred Grahamites are left within the remains of Revelation, and a good percentage of them are lined up in front of my shop holding cardboard boxes or canvas sacks. There is a sign hanging in the door that I can't read from the road.

"There you are," the last Grahamite in line says as I approach. He's the telephone sanitizer from Revelation. He takes a typewriter out of the cardboard box. "This thing still has memories. Your man was supposed to fix it. I want my money back."

The others are here for refunds too, and when I get to the head of the line, I see why they've all come today. The sign reads: "Closed 4 Business. Thanks for 15 Good Years."

"I promise, we aren't closing," I say to the people in line. "A misunderstanding with my business partner. Come back tomorrow, please, and I'll sort everything out."

I lock the door behind me, take down David's sign, and draw the drapes. I throw open the door to the workshop.

"Are you trying to ruin us?"

He wipes grease off his hands and steps away from what is no longer even recognizable as a hi-fi cabinet. Game Four of the '59 World Series blares from a wood-paneled radio. His smile is the same one I saw under the willows, the partitioned sunlight on his blotched skin.

"It's almost ready. After I fix things, you won't need me here any longer."

"Time travel doesn't work. Even if it did, I still need to make a living. Think of me for a minute."

He gestures to his machine. "I'll leave you what I've created. You'll be a very rich man. Then you'll find someone who can love you the way you deserve."

I put the pills down on the counter. "Take your medicine. Forget this impossible obsession."

"Don't you want me to be whole again?"

"We are whole. You can't change what happened that day,

David. You know where this all leads. I don't want to send you to Lakeshore, but I will if you give me no other choice."

That smile disappears. He backs away from me, touches his chest as if I kicked him. "That place is for sick people. I'm not sick. I've never seen more clearly."

I slam my open palm beside the pill bottle. "Take the damn drugs, then tell me if you still see clearly."

He nods as he reaches for the bottle. The safety seal makes a reassuring hiss. He pops a pill into his mouth and swallows. "No more talk of Lakeshore?"

I gesture to the clock radio from yesterday. "So long as there is no more talk about a time machine. Fix what you're good at. Tomorrow, I'm bringing in the Bel Air. It will keep us both busy and fed for at least a couple months."

"That sounds good. It's been a long time since I've worked on a car."

I watch him disassemble the clock radio. He works with the calm precision I've known from our years together. On the radio, the announcer for Game Four sounds like he is going insane: Chicago has just scored four runs at the top of the seventh, tying the game. The long-dead crowd roars.

The Bel Air will help, and so will the medicine. After my one and only visit to the hospital, I told myself that I would exhaust every avenue available before sending him to Lakeshore.

Music from the seventh inning stretch blares from the radio. David replaces the offending bulb with an old-fashioned incandescent and I slip out. The Backflasher is in my bag. I plop on the cerephones and start it up where I left off.

The lobby of Saint John the Baptist Secondary School. Pastor Kline gazing at his watch, Linda-Jane and Adam Mercer standing with him, both furious. I used to think Adam looked so old, but here, he looks exactly like the man I've worked and lived with these past fifteen years. The same grey eyes, receding hairline, strong jaw, sloping shoulders. Handsome, despite a weariness that reminds me of my mother's. Unlike David, Adam's skin is tanned a healthy bronze.

Why didn't we see it then?

"I stopped by Mrs. O'Leary's this morning," Linda-Jane says. "She didn't see either of you all night."

David doesn't look at his mother. He keeps his gaze on the Pastor. "Dr. Kline, I didn't see Mrs. O'Leary either. It's entirely possible we missed each other."

The Pastor looks up from his watch. "According to the Bible, which is worse: tardiness or bearing false witness?"

"Please don't kick me out," I say. "My mother will kill me, if the boys in my old school don't beat her to it. Please."

David squeezes my hand. "Billy Ray had nothing to do with this. Next semester we have to plan our Mission and I wanted to see the world beyond our walls to seek out my calling."

"And you found it?" Pastor Kline says.

David nods. "My Mission is clear."

"Are you feeling alright?" Linda-Jane says. "You look flushed. Did you drink any of the water out there?" She places a hand on David's forehead. He flinches at her touch. "You don't feel warm. How about rashes? Do you have any rashes?"

She reaches for the collar of his shirt. David steps away from her.

"To whom are you planning on Witnessing?" Pastor Kline says.

David smiles. "I have most of the details ironed out, but there are still a few wrinkles, and I would hate to present an incomplete thought. I'd be happy to submit a proposal to you by the end of the day."

The Pastor looks down at his watch again. "Until the end of the day then. Now get to class, you are late enough as is. And Billy Ray, don't let me catch you tardy again."

He steps out of our way to let us past. Adam Mercer grabs David as we rush by.

"Think hard on your Mission, son, and pray your thoughts are true."

David shrugs him off and we run down the hall. Before we go into Arithmetic, David pulls me aside.

"Ever since I was a boy, she's been checking me for rashes and spots. How could I have not seen this before?"

"My mom checks me for cancers and mega-measles all the

time."

He shakes his head and opens the door.

Anja and Rebecca sit between us and our desks. From the looks on their faces, the girls haven't gotten over the fact that we stole their clothes last night. Anja hisses "queers" as we pass, but Rebecca just stares at David.

The lesson is on Real Numbers. Even though I go back to this memory more than any other, I still don't know what I was supposed to learn that day. I spend the entire lecture looking at David, trying to make sure the disguise is working. He spends the entire class hunched over his notebook. When the bell rings, he shows me what he was working on: a web of interconnected names, his mother at the centre, and every man she's ever met scattered in bubbles around her, the connections between the different people drawn in pencil crayon.

"Any closer to figuring it out?" I say.

"It doesn't matter. Her sin must be revealed."

In the press of other students in the hall, I lose track of David. I'm still looking for him as I dial the combination for my locker. Anja pushes me into the metal door.

"That's for stealing my panties," she says. It's the first time anyone has rough-handled me since I transferred from the public schools. I flinch and prepare for the worst. "Hey, don't piss your jeans."

"I wasn't gonna. Have you seen David?"

"Your boyfriend ran off into the woods, probably to make out with 'Becca." Anja drapes an arm across my shoulder. "I've always wanted a queer friend."

"We're going to be late for Geography."

I squeeze away from her and run to a window. Green grass and playing fields stretch out to the banks of the Brightwater. There's no sign of him. Another bell rings for the start of class. I can't miss another, not with Kline breathing down my neck, so I sit behind my desk and fail to concentrate on another lesson.

David never makes it to class, and neither does Rebecca. Anja passes me notes criticizing the teacher's haircut. By lunch, the whole school buzzes with what has happened. I try to ignore the rumours. I want to hear it from my friend but they say he disappeared after it all went down. The afternoon stretches on for hours. The end of the day can't come fast enough. When it does, I run all the way to the gates of Revelation and out into Toronto.

I find David on the curb in front of my apartment. Make-up and filthy water have turned his school uniform to rags. He looks at me, lost, and I lead him to my mother's apartment.

I lean back in my chair behind the counter and breathe in the musty, stale air of the shop. The baseball game has ended, the Dodgers breaking the tie for the win, and now quiet hymns play in the workshop. He never went back to Revelation; he stayed with me from that day on. Our life hasn't been what either of us wanted, but we aren't hungry. We aren't alone.

Maybe we should take some time off, I think. Go somewhere. One of the lakes in Muskoka the public can still visit, or Parry Sound. We had a lovely time last summer on the beach near Parry Sound.

I open the door and peer in at David. He is wiring the clock radio into what was once the hi-fi cabinet and doesn't notice me enter. The pill bottle lies open on the workbench, empty. In the bathroom I find a single water-soaked pill floating in the centre of the toilet bowl.

"You flushed them? Do you know how much those pills cost?"

"They were poison, Billy Ray. I disposed of them accordingly."

I stare at him, trying to contain my rage. For a moment, I wish Pastor Kline hadn't seated me beside David. I wish that David hadn't found the Mothra sketch on my pencil case so interesting. Why couldn't I have fallen in love with another boy in high school, someone who could have spurned me, someone I could have forgotten?

I throw the pill bottle into the trash, stomp out of the workshop, and jog across the street toward what remains of Revelation. There's an old pay phone just outside the gate.

I ask the operator to connect me to Linda-Jane and Adam Mercer.

"Which community?" she asks in a perky soprano.

"Patience, or whatever you call the one outside Sudbury."

"Penitence. One moment please."

I lean against the warm bricks of Revelation's wall, waiting for the connection. I haven't been to the other side in fifteen years. David and I weren't the only ones who were expelled. Revelation's congregation decided that everything David's family had built was contaminated. Linda-Jane and Adam were shown the door, as was everything they built for Revelation. They floated from community to community until they found a more forgiving congregation up North. All the outside students were forbidden to attend John the Baptist Secondary School. They mothballed the water plant. Even Pastor Kline was evicted, as he'd known about the Mercer situation and had been complicit in covering up their sacrilege.

Instead of facing down the angry hordes in the public system, David and I found an online school that granted high school diplomas, and the two of us finished our schooling a year later in Mom's apartment. The cancer took her a couple months after graduation. She begged me to spend my meagre inheritance on university tuition. I used it on the first few months of rent for Billy Ray's Small Appliance Rehabilitation instead. It was David's idea, his way of helping Revelation rid itself of sacrilegious technology. We found an old computer repair shop across the street from Revelation and for fifteen years it's been home.

The line connects. "Linda-Jane speaking."

"I can't handle it anymore."

"Is that you, Billy Ray? Is David alright?"

"It's worse than the other times. He really thinks he can go back. He isn't eating."

"What about the medication?"

"He flushed it. I can't afford any more."

There's a muddled sound, muted voices, Linda-Jane holding her hand over their old-style receiver.

"Why don't we drive down there? He's our son."

"We both know he won't see you. It will be worse than last time."

Another delay, as she relays what I said. An old Pontiac rolls through the gate in the wall and belches black smoke as it accelerates down the street.

"So why are you calling?"

"Lakeshore Hospital will take him," I say. "But I can't afford it. He'll get good care there. They specialize in Bernard's Syndrome."

She doesn't bother covering the receiver this time: "He needs money, to send David to that hospital."

I can't make out Adam's response over the din of the traffic.

"If he gets the treatment," she says to me. "Do you think he'll agree to see us?"

"I think so," I say. "Once he's better, of course he'll want to see you."

She likes my little lie. It will take time, she says, to put together that much money. Another mortgage, and then they'll have to get the Grahamite bank in Sudbury to make the transfer. I tell her I can cover the hospital fees in the meantime. All I have to do is get him there.

The hardest part will be getting him in the car. I phone Dr. LaRose to let her to know I will be coming; she doesn't sound surprised. The afternoon sun bakes the asphalt as I hurry back to the shop.

David is putting away his tools. He smiles as I enter.

"It's finished," he says, and gestures to his creation. The hi-fi cabinet forms the heart around which the rest of the device has congealed. Two chairs are tacked to the front of the cabinet, and cerephones hang from the backrests of both chairs. The cerephones are wired into the mass of resistors, vacuum tubes, and capacitors tied in to an old telephone switchboard, at the top of which sits my Backflasher. "All I need is your help, and I can belong again."

I nod, trying to be reasonable.

"The Bel Air is almost fit to drive," I say. "It just needs a bit of tweaking. They should have it here this evening. We should really clear this out to make room."

He taps the slim metal box of the Backflasher. "Aren't you curious, Billy Ray?"

Curious doesn't even begin to describe it. David isn't supposed to use technology like the Backflasher; what is it doing sitting in his machine?

"The Bel Air will be here soon. Why don't we move this out of the way and you can tell me how it works."

He indicates one of the two chairs attached to his machine. "Sit, please. This won't take long."

The Backflasher controller is attached to the arm of the chair he indicated, but he's tacked new controls onto it: they look like buttons from an old reel-to-reel machine. Play, forward, reverse, and a big red button that he's drawn an X through.

"I just don't see how we will fit the car in here," I say.

"I'm not doing anything until I've made things right," he says. "But I can't do it without you. I'm forbidden to operate your Backflasher. With it, we can go back to the day I ruined everything, and you can make it disappear."

"Backflashers don't work that way; they can't delete memories."

"This isn't a Backflasher. The past only exists in our minds, isn't that what you've always told me? This can delete the past, therefore this is a time machine." He pats the seat beside him. "Do this for me, Billy Ray. Let me belong again."

I can't stop staring at the red button with the X through it. Every option, that's what I told myself. I sit in the chair. He hands me the control panel. I slip on the cerephones while he straps himself in.

"Take us back," he says.

So I do, back to the morning after David's Shift, as we file out of Arithmetic class.

Students crowd into the hallway of John the Baptist Secondary School. Up ahead, a younger version of me walks to my locker. I watch through David's eyes, experiencing more than just David's vision. I live his memory. He has contrived a way to share the Backflasher experience. That discovery alone could make us wealthy, but all I can think about is how the young David feels as he looks over at the young version of myself. He pities me. After seeing where I live, and despite everything I've done to help him, he pities me, because I don't really belong in his community.

When Anja comes up behind the younger me, David sneaks over to the door and slips outside, across the playing fields, toward the Brightwater. Thoughts rush in a wild torrent through his mind. Ideas and sensations and doubts and analyses shout in a cacophony that reminds me of the clatter in Union Station at rush hour. It's only after half a minute of careful listening that I can discern dominant themes in his busy mind: righteous indignation and strong purpose. He's convinced of his mother's crimes and he knows exactly how to expose her.

As he reaches the bank of the Brightwater, I hear a disembodied voice speaking in my right ear.

"Every detail is exactly as I remember it," the older David says. I open my eyes and see him superimposed over the willows that line the bank, the senior David strapped to his chair, eyes clenched shut. "I don't know why you require this crutch."

"It's entertainment," I say, closing my eyes, returning to his memories.

"This is where you start the deletion."

The young David passes the Baptismal Pools and emerges on the neatly cut grass surrounding the water treatment plant. The gardener is a younger Mr. Ussander. He pulls weeds from beneath the roses and waves as David jogs past. David notices every detail as he runs: the number of weeds and the number of roses and the ratio of one to the other, an estimate of the hour based on the filtration plant's shadow, a precise calculation of the flow rate of the water exiting the plant. His Brainy Baby mind is shifting into something unrecognizable, yet even with his enhanced powers of perception, he can't see what he is becoming.

The treatment plant is two stories of red brick and grey concrete. David hammers on the main entrance door until an operator in coveralls opens it.

"Adam Mercer," David says. "Bring him out here at once."

"You're his boy, aren't you? Something the matter?"

"Just bring him here."

The door clangs shut. David paces, rehearsing the accusation he'll deliver to the man he is certain has also been betrayed by his mother. This close to the wall, the hot asphalt and urine stink of the city fills the air, but mingled with it comes the perfume from the rose garden and the cool scent of clean, flowing water. David walks past the '37 Ford pickup being loaded with bottles to the dammed reservoir that marks the end of the polluted Highland Creek.

Adam Mercer steps out into the warm morning, his tanned skin dark against his white Oxford. David calls his name from the banks of the reservoir, and then he wades down into the filthy water flowing in from the city.

"What are you doing, son?" Adam says.

"All of this must go," the older David sitting beside me says.

"She made a fool of you," the young David says. His thoughts still rage, spilling the banks of their old channels, but he holds on to anything that feels like certainty. "And she made an abomination of me."

He dunks his arms into the oily water. Make-up dissolves, revealing forearms covered in Bernie Blotches.

"Get out of there," Adam says. "You don't understand anything."

Plant workers follow Adam to the banks of the reservoir. They line up behind him, watching the boy in the water. Only then does David lend more weight to the currents of doubt flowing through his mind. In an instant he realizes his mistake.

"Go back inside," Adam says to the workers.

The gardener drops his tools and joins more plant workers as they gather behind Adam. David's father stares at the crowd for a moment, then slides down the bank. Adam rolls up the sleeve on his shirt. David already knows that the skin beneath will be covered in Bernie Blotches.

"You're the one," David says. He grabs his father's hand. "You made me this."

"I've learned how to live with who I am," Adam says. "Let me teach you. We can still belong."

David pulls his father into the reservoir.

As Adam rises sputtering, Rebecca rounds the corner of the filtration plant. She tows Pastor Kline behind her. Water streams off Adam's face, taking the bronze tan with it, and revealing clusters of Bernie Blotches similar to David's.

"See, Dr. Kline," Rebecca says. "I told you something was wrong with him."

Kline shakes his head. The plant workers gathered on the bank stare at the man who built the plant in which they work.

"This doesn't change who we are," Adam says to the Grahamites above him. "We are still faithful."

David pushes away from his father. All the hatred he's reserved for his mother doubles in intensity. They both did this to him. His mother didn't have an affair with a Bernie Baby, she married one and snuck him into Revelation. They defiled him before he was born and condemned him to a life that guaranteed eternal damnation.

"You did this," he says to his father. He faces Rebecca. "Tell them it's not my fault."

Rebecca takes the Pastor's hand. "'Come ye out from among them,'" she says.

The workers seem to emerge from their mute amazement at the oft-repeated words.

"'And be ye separate,'" they say with one voice.

Rebecca turns her back on David and his father. The workers do the same. Pastor Kline remains, staring down at the father and son in the water.

"Please, Kline," Adam says. "You knew this day might come. Help us go back to how it was."

"'And touch not the unclean thing," the pastor says, and he too turns his back.

"This is our home," Adam says.

They walk away, none of them looking back at us. Only the gardener, Mr. Ussander, remains, shaking his head a moment, before he returns to his roses. David shudders in the tepid water. He knows what the ritual words of the shunning mean. He swims across the reservoir toward the culvert that lets the filthy stream through the wall.

"Son, please," Adam says. "Let me help you."

"Save yourself."

David dives. He swims against the current, pulling himself along the ribbed walls of the culvert, until he surfaces outside Revelation. David blinks through the caustic liquid, the towers of Toronto an unnavigable maze in a foreign country. Then he remembers that there is one person outside Revelation's walls who still loves him.

"Here," the other David says, the one strapped in beside me. "Cut everything to here."

I open my eyes and look at the basic controls he built. The young David drags himself out of the water, past a rotting cat and a rusting dishwasher.

"Do it now," the senior David says. "Cut this out of me, Billy Ray. I'll never belong if I remember what I did."

"You belong here," I say. I can still hear the birds singing on the other side of the wall. David's whole life lies exposed before me, pinned to a table, and I am the surgeon tasked with excising the tumour. He's wanted this for so long, how can I deny it?

"What's the delay?"

"I was praying."

"You never pray."

I adjust the controls, I make the incision. David lets out a breath and slumps forward in his chair. His breathing is irregular, and he makes tiny whimpering sounds, a young child having a nightmare. In my mind, I see him rise from the chair only to find this hole in his memory, this absence around which he's revolved for so long. The hole will become the pivot of a new Fascination. The Bel Air won't be enough to keep his mind busy. David needs a project he can work on for the rest of his life.

One of the cerephones pops off David's lolling head. I pluck the other off and sit back down in my chair. I would try everything before sending him to live at Lakeshore, but until today I didn't know what everything entailed.

I place the second set of cerephones to my forehead and activate the Backflasher. My whole life stretches out before me, my surgeon's tools still bloody. I stare at it for a long time, unsure of where to make the final cut.

David begins to stir. He looks so much like his father.

"Take your medicine," I say, and I press the big red X.

Pine-scented wind sweeps the beach.

Little snow daggers cut my face at the streetcar stop outside Lakeview Hospital.

David and I push a restored icebox out of the shop and it slips off the cart and cracks on the concrete floor.

Thunderheads roll above the city as David shows me a machine he claims will undo his greatest sin.

Mom's skin is so soft after she stops breathing.

Laughter on opening the envelopes that contain our high school graduation diplomas.

Willow-partitioned sunlight across David's bare chest.

Geoffrey W. Cole's award-winning short fiction has appeared in such publications as *Apex*, *Clarkesworld*, *EscapePod*, *New Worlds*, and *Imaginarium 2012: The Year's Best Canadian Speculative Writing*. His stories have been translated into Catalan, French, Hungarian, Italian, Romanian, and Spanish, and have been produced as podcasts. He is the 2016 winner of the Premis Ictineu for best story translated into Catalan. Geoff has degrees in biology, engineering, and an MFA in creative writing from the University of British Columbia. He lives with his wonderful wife, three sons, and giant hound in Toronto, Canada. Geoff is a member of SF Canada and SFWA. Visit Geoff at www.geoffreywcole.com.

Unnatural Selection

Tim Fab-Eme

You must know Darwin—not any darwin
in forums with telescopes on his eyes
always singing the beard like a puppet,
or one having his tag by accident;
I really mean the God of chance—
he respected me, no, he deified me
not because I once mirrored his incubation
when we sat alone on HMS Beagle,
but that I surpassed him in jest—

this, too, he dismissed when I reviewed
the *Origin* **long before it absorbed us.**
I had asked as throes gripped him,
what he would be after the time—
My friend, he called, *there is no death*
but transmutation, and we laughed at sophistry.
So, Darwin never died as you presume,
and not only he, but every extinct thing:

do not compose elegies for *Tiktaalik roseae,*
dinosaurs, *Raphus cucullatus* **and golden toads**
or remind me of Suyá and Ostrogoth,
St. Helena olives and Sri Lanka legumes—
they have, indeed, been transformed—I know
he would agree wherever whatever he is,
that the Holocene extinction is natural selection.

He knew I detest praising friends privately,
I sing them loud as a thrush
I laud public approval, which he adored,
and I told him in undressed words
that I did not share his lust
and how he swore in the name

of greed and in its night-birthed misnomers
we give all the things that limp
backwards into the beautiful door of love;
the stubble smiled and laughed at me,
yet he did not stir my head

to make differently how we should live.
I never meant, friend, to distract you,
to cut new pathways in your mind
to discredit or credit the new whiskers,

and believe me, I wonder every day
as I walk across shacks and skyscrapers
how many of us daily go extinct

by our fatal greed and inverse love
that wet the long lungs of death—

and which of us, Malthus, is next?

Niger Delta Blues

Tim Fab-Eme

You don't know what it means to live unknown,
to smile in the market square as a stranger
haughtily spills your mother's name on a pig's head
and you become a boil on Miss World's lips.
This is how a mangrove lives without prop roots:

a branch is starved until its pregnant leaves become
ghosts of IDPs walking backwards to Oloibiri Well 1.
def.: Oloibiri is the longing of a surrogate mum
e.g.: She died birthing crude oil for the outsiders.

You don't know how it feels when a foe
owns your child and you bow calling him, *Lord*,
while your neighbours cut your neck with snail shells;

you can't protest because your life's a nursery rhyme
of CH_4 NOx VOCs SO_2 CO_2 PAHs PCBs HFCs

and the other poisons that eat me away daily.

Tim Fab-Eme experiments with poetic forms; he writes about exploitation, identity and the environment. His work has appeared in *The Malahat Review*, *New Welsh Review*, *FIYAH* and *Magma*, et cetera. Tim often turns to reggae, highlife and jazz whenever the news weighs him down. He studied engineering at the Niger Delta University, and when he isn't working on control instruments, he picks a book and buries himself in it. Tim will soon join the University of Port Harcourt for a BA in English; he lives in Rivers, Nigeria.

Growing Roots

Alan Bao

1.

When the shuttle left the ionosphere, Abby Huang saw bands of light playing across the poles. The earth filled up half of the silicate window, a shrinking, light-blue horizon. Abby had looked at the receding planet in the distance, and thought to herself:

That tiny blue ball—that's Home. That's Everything.

There was a moment of awesome spiritual terror.

Then she covered up the window with her palm and pushed the blue-green planet out of her mind.

"Xiaolu, you shouldn't complain," her father once told her. He called her Xiaolu—never by her anglicized name, even though she'd often pleaded with him to do so in front of her American friends. *"This is where you're from. This is home."*

She was fifteen. The air was sticky and smelled of petrol. The humidity made it difficult to breathe. Wading through the smog and heat, she could not resist the urge to pick at the acne and neon-red sweat rashes that blossomed across her face. *Shui tu bu fu,* her grandparents had called it—the rejection of a foreign body by the water and earth—or, the rejection of the water and earth by a foreigner's body. Abby walked head-down along the pagoda walkways, trying painfully to keep out of the sightlines of passers-by.

"Xiaolu, do you know what the difference between a water-lily and a water-hyacinth is?" Her father asked, pointing at the pond below. She shook her head, deftly hiding her face as a group of cute boys padded by, laughing with the easy swagger of tourists. Her father was a serious man—he did not like parties or MTV or pop music, or

any of the things that she liked to gossip to her friends about back home in Oregon. Their conversations would always return to the same thing: the plants, the biology; the work he could never leave at work.

Abby sighed. A crescent day-moon sat like a splash of chalk in the watergarden below. She listened disinterestedly as her father waxed on about stolons and root systems, while *laowai* and tourists swarmed through New Chenghuang Temple's stifling heat.

"...more importantly, water-lilies anchor themselves with roots below the waterline, while the water-hyacinths are all free-floating plants..."

She stood and stared and said nothing. They leaned over the water and lazed in the Puxi swelter, glo-cubes lighting up one by one as the sun crawled lower in the sky.

That was before the cold war—back when all those things still existed. Abby supposed they must still be down there somewhere, on that fragile shred of blue that used to be home—but they were not for her. Her world was now one of underground tunnels and water rations; of wet-wipes and recycled fluids, and the sterile-white of lunar dust. The earth was just a satellite, a distant blue moon above a humbling sweep of desolation, floating like a waterflower in an endless black ocean.

She'd made her own watergarden on the moon.

No—that was not entirely true. Ownership was such an earthly idea—a conceptual luxury that had no place on Luna. Better to say that she'd simply made a piece of home for herself where it wouldn't have otherwise existed. The colony's patchwork of edible reeds and algae vats were reminders of happier days—iso-sealed and humid, like a Puxi summer. There used to be an entire team of eight working in hydroponics, but Abby was the only one left now: the sole curator of the colony's living greenhouse, maintaining and calibrating the ancient equipment, making sure that the algae stores continued to pump out vital oxygen for their precious little foothold of life on the moon.

The comm-line blipped on her shoulder.

"Abs, I missed you at dinner. Are you working late again?"

She fumbled with her equipment, trying to wipe the grease off her fingers.

"That busy, huh? Listen, I'll bring some food down. You were sick all morning; you really should take some time off."

Abby sighed. Her free hand found her stomach. The data-tag blipped under her thumb as she ticked off another hydroponic vat from the maintenance checklist. Number sixty-six was a geriatric old thing, prone to leakage and rust—an outdated hunk of equipment that would have been replaced years ago, had the earthbound governments been able to tear their teeth from each other's throats long enough to mind the moon.

She cracked out her aching back and bobbed through the aisles of silver-gray machinery. Her thoughts veered back towards glo-cubes and Puxi summers, and to their little house in Oregon, before the war, before their relocation to the federal camps. She came to an unsteady stop past the pH equalizers, gripping the sides of a tiny water-tank and feeling its cold, metallic frame against her palms. There, in front of her, was the jewel in the crown of her little empire: one cubit foot of still water, crowded over with lilies and hyacinths.

"Abby. *There* you are."

Abby started from her thoughts. She had not heard the doors.

"Fishing for glo-flies again?"

Abby laughed and held up her grease-stained work cloth. *Just taking a break*, she gestured. John bobbed over to her and sidled up close, stealing a kiss from the corner of her lips. He pushed a stew-tube into her hand, and pulled out a vacuum-pack for himself.

"Brought you some food."

"Thanks," she said, peering into the water tank, stretching out the knots in her muscles. The surface looked much too dark for only one cubic foot of water. "I was just thinking about home. You know it'll be eight years this November since we've been up here?"

"Longer, for me." John ran his fingers across the lilies on the surface. He'd been among the first wave of domestic protesters to speak out against the federal surveillance program, and had lost his house and his job for his un-Americanism. Not quite a *them,* in the partisan sense of things—but something just as frightening: an invisible shadow of sedition, without even the basic decency to be visibly distinguishable from the *us*; a cancer of un-patriotism that could not be allowed to speak freely in the land of the free.

"You Chinese get all your censorship from your government, while we in America are expected to do it ourselves." John once said, back when he and Abby first met. Back then, he was the immaculate portrait of the bitter exile: a sneering young man with a inexhaustible wellspring of cynicism, whose words always sounded way too old for his age. When they met in the hallways, his stance was always guarded—shoulders up, head down—engaging in perfunctory conversation with the enemy alien, whose foreignness was only blunted by their shared predicament.

But as things go, Luna had a way of breaking earthly presumptions. The moon gathered people like them: floating water-flora of questionable loyalty, unable to root in the tensile, suspicious world below. They had flitted out of the ionosphere like glo-flies, even as all the scientists of sturdy nationalistic allegiance scrambled to get home in time for the thermonuclear holocaust.

John snapped open a vacuum pack and waved it under her nose. She gasped at the familiar, tangy smell.

"Dried fruit? *Real* fruit?"

He smiled and nodded.

"Paul gave them out at mess. Good haul this cycle. UNJO-funded."

Abby brought a fig to her mouth and bit down, feeling the seeds crunch and pop through their sticky-sweet insides.

"It must be thawing out down there."

"Must be." John shrugged, popping some raisins into his mouth. Abby frowned at that. He was too non-committal about earth politics, these days. Surely, the thawing of tensions down below was good news for exiles like them.

"Anyway, how much do you still have to do?"

She looked around the room and groaned. There were still twenty out of the eighty-six water-silos that she had not yet checked up on. Between those and her scheduled isometrics, she'd be lucky to get a wink of sleep before reveille.

John seemed to be able to read her thoughts.

"You're sick in the mornings and tired at night. You're working too hard, Abs. Just skip the isometrics for a day, will you?"

Abby sighed. Once again, her free hand found her stomach, strolling over the smoothweave fabric of her clothes. She sucked down the stew tube and finished up the last of the maintenance work with John peering helpless and impatient over her shoulders. They lugged her equipment down the halls, bouncing and bobbing into the walls until they parted ways at the isometrics room.

She watched John's retreating back through the hallway. Perhaps it was her imagination, or the fluorescent lighting saturating the walls—but she could not help thinking that, in this light, he looked much thinner than usual.

2.

Morning reveille was at 7:00 AM, Lunar Standard. The corridors' artificial lights flickered into slow-glow, a pale fluorescent facsimile of the terran sunrise. Abby was up and moving an hour before the music seeped through the speakers in its rising tune.

For breakfast: a tube of nutrient paste and another of simulated oatmeal that she'd left out to thaw the night before. She downed them quickly, over the protest of nausea in her stomach. A glass of re-condensed water went down stale and tinny, and then her daily steroids and calcium tablets, before she bobbed down the lightening halls towards the isometric rooms.

The isometrics were the closest thing she had to religion on Luna. The exercise room was her steeple; the ranging lunges, her dogma. It was a sweating and heaving congregation, in daily prayer that the earth wouldn't crush the life out of their de-calcified bones once they returned to its gravity. It was the one thing that told the home-bound apart from the lifers—the Scrawnies and Lunies that talk show hosts joked about on primetime Earthnet.

Stretch-heave.

She gave her musculature a testing flex, strutting her full range of motion against the cables. She could tune out the creak of the straining machines, the heavy breathing of the other attendees, and the scent of evaporating sweat being sucked into moisture collectors. The contractions of tensile wireframes stretched into spiritual nihilism, as mind-erasing as Buddhist zen.

Stretch-heave.

In her vision: a sweep of dancing lights from the ionosphere, and the afterglow of a receding horizon.

Stretch-heave.

A fragile splash of blue in an all-black sky.

Stretch-heave.

Waterflowers in a Puxi haze.

Before the cold war, she had been an American. Pretty-faced and tall for her age. Perpetually heartbroken and happy, the way teenagers are.

She had been content in their little Oregonian suburb, among the quiet houses and the trees and the suburban, two-lane streets. She liked the schools and the people, the pizza and gossip at familiar hangouts. She liked the dances and the Oregonian boys, who fawned after her like exotic spices from a faraway land. Disquieting, in its own way—though, truth be told, she'd always rather liked the attention.

"You're lucky you're pretty and popular, you know. They can be so cruel to us sometimes."

The only other immigrant family had lived ten miles outside of town. Their child Bo was a freshman, one year her junior, whose parents had gone through painful lengths to enrol him in a richer school. She understood their obsession with scholastic prestige because of her father—but she also knew that, well-intentioned though they were, they hadn't done the boy any favours. He was a shy kid, quiet and shabby, who could not keep up in sports or conversations. He ate his lunches alone in a stairwell in the disused north wing of the school, and she'd laughed dutifully along with her friends whenever the popular boys tormented him in the hallways.

With her, he seemed to forgive readily.

"We're not the same as them," he said once, sitting on their porch, nursing a split lip for talking back to Bobby Lee at school the week before. Her father had forced her to stay at home while he hosted the boy's parents. "I don't think we'll ever be."

In the shade of suburban awnings, looking out at the middle-class cul-de-sac, Bo's accented speech and deliberate use of '*we*' sounded out of place. The boy bothered her; everything from his shabby clothes, to his imposition of camaraderie, to his half-smiling way of speaking, as if he was letting on less than he knew.

Abby had last heard from him when they shipped him to the federal camps for un-Americanism. The injustice of it sat like lead in her stomach. Flexing against her binding cables, she wondered at how quickly the earth had become such an unhappy place.

Stretch-heave.

The fluorescence of the isometric room came back and heliographed before her eyes. She felt a churning in her belly, cresting in a familiar wave of nausea.

Stretch-heave.

She dropped the cables and clutched at her stomach.

Vomit fell slowly in 1/6 G.

3.

"Your viral and bacterial screens came back negative."

The pronouncement was as cold as a scalpel. Abby shifted uncomfortably as Dr. Stelman, one of the colony's two bag-eyed, overworked doctors, frowned from the datapad to his patient.

The sterile whiteness of the room stifled her.

"You know I can't give out anything without a solid diagnosis. Things are tight enough as it is."

Abby contorted her neck into a nod, doing her best to ignore the anxiety that crept down her spine and tingled in her toes. Luna, she knew, was not the sort of place you wanted to fall ill. The med-lab had countermeasures for the most common lunar ailments; Zalmatox courses for immunodeficiency, steroids for muscle atrophy, cal-tabs for osteopenia, even a needlewire electrolysation kit for aortic calcification . . . But at the end of the day, the long list of things that could go wrong with a human body in 1/6 G was nowhere near exhaustive. The colony was barely a generation old—new complications were still popping out of the woodwork on a consistent basis, sending bodies to the waste dump and leaving med-staff puzzled and helpless.

Dr. Stelman pressed at her belly, giving her a start.

"What about your periods?" he asked. "Have they been regular?"

There was a beat of silence. Then Abby almost laughed out loud. She looked at the doctor, searching his face for the twinkle of a joke, but found only tired and humourless eyes. She shrugged helplessly. Her periods had been irregular ever since she came to Luna—reproductive complications and sterility were common side effects of long-term extraterrestrial life. Luna was a population built on immigrants alone; birth rates were the sole purview of terran statisticians.

Dr. Stelman stared at the datapad, brows furrowed in consternation.

"We'll do an ultrasound, just to be sure." He murmured. "That's probably not it, but still . . . ."

John had been as surprised as she when he got the news.

"They want to do *what*?" He'd half-laughed as he bobbed uncertainly towards the pulled bed-frame.

Now, as the rising crescendo of lights and reveille music seeped across the halls, Abby could only watch with a pang of homesickness as her usual congregation filed out of the isometrics room. She nodded to the regulars as she bobbed past. John had appealed to his shift manager to accompany her to the test, but as per usual with the colony's strapped work shifts, the response had been curt and practical: *"Pregnancies don't happen off-planet. Stelman's been working too hard lately. You know we can't give time off for trivial things."*

Abby sighed. Trivial things.

Next to the weight of the moon, everything was trivial.

"Hey Huang. No isos today?"

Abby shook her head and bounced by wordlessly. The woman laughed and slapped her on the rump, a little over-friendly in her endorphin high.

"You'd better not be going native, lady."

Overhead, the fluorescent lights had reached their full

brightness. The halls began to fill with activity as the lifers and homebound alike made from their dorms and began their daily buzz around the colony. Abby's stomach bounced with every bobbing step. The nausea-suppressants she took from the med lab seemed to be working, at least. She made her way through the winding corridors towards medical, past hydroponics, past the branching northern hall that led the waste disposal unit on the far side of the colony. She'd taken a work-shift there, back when she first landed. Mostly bio-tox and bodies—archiving the ID tags of the dead and reclaiming the moisture from their bodies, before sealing the airlock and letting the pressure gradient carry the husks down the poop chute. Some of the bodies would roll and be carried by their own inertia over a crater rim. Most of them just laid there in the lunar dust and debris, shrunken and glossy-eyed, never decaying.

She'd had her own brief rebellion at the thought of drying and dumping the dead, instead of burying them—but that phase had been mercifully short-lived. Earth-born sentimentalism did not last long on Luna.

Dr. Stelman greeted her curtly as she entered the med-lab. She watched from outside her body as the assistant prepped the electrodes and laid her down on the worn polystyrene table.

"Don't be so nervous," came the scripted reassurance. "It's probably nothing. Just a routine test."

Abby almost laughed at the absurdity of it all. Routine? For whom? She thought of earthly mothers in their bracing gravity, complaining about hospital foods and commute times and the noisy birds outside. She thought of what it would be like to eat fresh foods, to feel natural humidity on her skin, to be able to unironically think of life as a blessing, rather than some vaguely fearful variable in the annals of space exploration.

As the gel-tipped sensor glided cool and ticklish across her skin, Abby Huang closed her eyes and lost herself to thoughts of home.

"Finally. I thought we'd never get out of airport security. How many times do they have to grope a girl before they're convinced she's not some

bomb-strapped Manchurian candidate?"

In the distant past, Abby's father was laughing, ushering a visiting Chinese couple to the living room. Their little Oregonian suburb sat in a haze of weekend ennui, sunlight flooding the house through their venetian blinds.

(The coolness of the ultrasound gel tickled her abdomen).

"Things have been tense since the Strait of Japan incident... Sorry it was such a hassle for you to get here. I hope people can come to their senses soon and not let things escalate any further."

The woman nodded in agreement, shaking hands with her father for the twentieth time, laughing and dropping her glottals in a twanging Ningbo accent. The man smiled with aloof politeness. It was familiar scene in the Huang household: her father and his colleagues, sitting around the coffee table, waxing political about the latest international developments over a pot of chrysanthemum tea and a bowl of oily American snacks.

Abby observed the grown-ups as she snacked idly in the kitchen.

"Still, not the best time for visiting America, eh, Da Huang?" said the woman. *"The TSA aside, I heard a few of your colleagues got into trouble with the university for un-Americanism."*

"Ah, Liu Bu. He's never been the type who could leave his politics at home."

The woman nodded, then threw up her shoulders in the universal *what-can-you-do* gesture.

"That's how it starts, isn't it? It's the same everywhere. The screws are being tightened on the mainland, too. My friend from internal says there's even talk of revoking all American business visas, if the US sanctions go ahead."

"And a good job of it, if that," interjected the man from the other end of the couch. His tone was terse and confrontational, cutting through the Sunday haze. Abby perked up from her Cheetos. Maybe something interesting would happen, after all.

The woman shot her companion a cold warning glance. Abby's father only shrugged.

"I'm sure it won't come to that."

"Well, if it does, it'll be your *American jingoism that provoked it. We would've settled the issue with Little Japan years ago—*you're *the ones butting into regional politics where you don't belong...."*

"Damn it, honey, let's not do this again...."

Abby peeked surreptitiously over her snack-bag at the grown-ups in the other room. Something about the man's deliberate use of pronouns unsettled her. Abby knew nothing about the rising tensions in the Straits of Japan, or the nationalistic media clampdown at Xinhua, or the hawkish electoral rhetoric being spewed on Capitol Hill—but, looking at her father, all laugh lines and a neatly-parted businessman's cut over his traditional Han features, she could not help but wonder who they were supposed to be in this scenario—the 'you' or the 'we'?

"You know, you should really watch CCTV sometime—it would be a change of pace from your imperialist American news. Why, just a week ago, Lin Xiaochen ran a segment highlighting the provocative American foreign policy...."

Abby's father waved his hand, as if slapping away an insect.

"Lin Xiaochen! That old demagogue salivates over the idea of war as if it were a spectator sport."

"Spoken like an un-patriotic coward. When your country's security and dignity is on the line, it's your duty *to fight!"*

The man accentuated the word 'fight' with a solid smack on the knee. The female guest sat in her seat, rubbing her temple in mute, resigned embarrassment. Abby's father nodded coldly.

"Let the demagogues whinge and roar. You can bet that it won't be them or their children enlisting to fight, if war ever did break out."

The man set down his teacup with an audible clink.

"If war ever did break out, I'd *send* my *son to fight."*

There was an uncomfortable silence.

Abby sighed and returned to her Cheetos.

In the present, Dr. Stelman narrowed his eyes, squinting at the grainy screen of the ultrasound. The electric thrum of two parallel heartbeats filled Abby's world with equal parts wonder and dread.

"Anyhow, I think you're out of touch, Mr. Huang," the man said, as the suburban tableau scattered like a breaking mosaic. *"All you get here is American news, American rhetoric. Plenty of* patriotic *Chinese agree with me."*

The scent-memory of chrysanthemums hung in the air.

4.

"A baby? Is it true, Xiaolu, you're having a baby?"

The comm-link blared like a runaway train. Abby smiled a little vindictively, thinking of the federal censors listening in on their line, probably grasping their coffees and cringing against the excited noise.

"Ma, please don't gush. It's a bit more complicated than that."

Abby tried to smile back through the screen. She wondered how to convey the precariousness of her situation without upsetting her beaming mother; how to express the four hundred thousand kilometres of distance between her child and the life-giving earth; the political complications of her status if she were to ever return; the weeks of hushed, tearful debates between herself and John over whether to keep the child at all. Dr. Stelman's sterile, professional words rang in her head:

"There have never been any studies on the effects of a lunar environment on human pregnancy. We'll monitor the situation carefully, but bear in mind that there's no guarantee that the child will come to term . . . ."

Her mother bounded back through the transmission lag:

"Oh, who's gushing, Xiaolu? I'm just so glad to see your face again. When the government men told us, we didn't believe them. But then the news started talking about it, and then even the army folks guarding the camp—and when they told us that we'd be able to see you again, after all these years . . . !" Wiping tears from her eyes, she continued: "I'm so happy for you. You know there isn't a person on earth who isn't rooting for you, Xiaolu!"

Abby smiled and took that with a grain of salt—but she had to admit that the first communiqués from earth *had* been heartening. The near-defunct UN Joint Operations office had gotten in touch with both the Chinese and American authorities, who had in turn located her mother in one of the internment centers and set up a weekly supervised line directly from Luna into camp. At mess, Paul had showed them clip after clip of optimistic terran pundits pointing out the reconciliatory symbolism of the moon-child in a thawing political landscape. And when Joint Operations ran their social media Q&A, the longest-running thread on Earthnet had been an outpouring of congratulations from both sides of the Great

Firewall—though, she had to remind herself in her moments of overt optimism, the second-longest had been an ongoing wiki-limerick titled "The Turncoat and the Chinky Whore."

"I'm really happy to hear that, Ma. How are things at the, uh—" She paused, re-assessing her words. 'Internment camp' was still a taboo phrase in the federal lexicon. "—how are things at the assembly center?"

If her mother picked up on her unease, she didn't show it.

"Oh, we've mostly been talking about you, Xiaolu! We had a dance last week to celebrate the news. Bo fixed up one of the old farmhouses, the supervising officer approved it, and everybody in the camp showed up and danced. Even some of the army guards came out to join us—what were their names again . . . ?"

"That—that's great, Ma!" Abby yelled, cutting her mother off before she could blurt them out. A bit of camaraderie between guards and internees was one thing; but openly fraternizing with interned aliens was still big trouble, even in the thawing world below.

Then, something else clicked in the back of her head:

"Wait, ma, did you say Bo?"

"Yes! Oh, but you wouldn't know! He was transferred here after you left for Patriot School! He's here now, in the other room. Silly boy, he said he didn't want to intrude on our time. Xiao Bo, come out here!"

Abby watched in astonishment as the boyish face came sliding on-screen, carrying an uncharacteristic dry smirk. That Bo would somehow end up in the same camp as her mother was not unheard of—persons certified as 'low-threat' were routinely put in the same re-settlements as their old neighbours. What surprised her was the fact that he was still there. He had been even younger than she was when they interned him, and she could not imagine that he would have any reason to stay.

"Hey, Xiaolu." He laughed. "You look a little shocked to see me."

She gave a little wave into the comm-screen.

"I'm *happy* to see you, Bo—I just didn't expect you to be in a camp, of all places. I thought for sure you would have taken the Patriot Exams by now!"

"That garbage?" He laughed.

Abby bit her tongue. Surely he knew it was a supervised line?

"Like I'd lie and pander just to get out." He grinned wider. There was a tinge of desperation in it. "And anyway, I not a naturalized American, remember? I never had the option in the first place."

John nodded knowingly from his corner. The Naturalized Child Citizens Act had applied only to American-born aliens, giving them the option to be housed and re-educated elsewhere, away from their families in the camps. When the choice had been extended to Abby, her mother had asked no questions, only kissed her on the forehead and wished her the best.

"You can have a life and a future, Abby," she'd said—a way out from the group bunks and unpartitioned washrooms of the camp; a tantalizing whiff of freedom that had stolen into the oubliette where they'd been stored and forgotten. A few years away in some government boarding school had seemed like a small price to pay.

Abby sighed and remembered a trip they took during her Patriot years—a tour of some university in the mid-west, shepherded under the shadows of neo-Georgian buildings for a glimpse of the world that they would one day inhabit as productive Patriots. Their supervising chaperones had marched them openly across the quad, and she'd felt the eyes of passersbys upon their little clique: hack musicians handing out flyers, ultimate-frisbee-ers fighting over a drink, friends out for a spring picnic on the grass; all craning their necks to stare as they passed by. And Abby watched them in her turn, her eyes connecting with theirs through a great distance, wondering at the lives and dreams of those other people from that other world.

The memory made her sad. Those were the days when she still belonged to earth—when she still believed that the other world had a place for her. Over time, she grew to be inured to the hostile looks from strangers in the streets, to the slurs and snide remarks that led to workplace altercations, and to the termination notices from mediators as they invariably sided with her harassers. She went through her days in a haze, bouncing from one potential employer to the next, watching them squint at her Patriot certificate as though searching for forgery. Some days, she found herself becoming inexplicably angry at even her own friends: their offers of financial support became jeers of superiority; their sympathetic, *I'm-sorry-you-had-to-go-through-that* pep-talks became increasingly underwritten by the unspoken implication, "I *would never have to."* Holding her rancour out at arm's length, she grew to hate the broke, angry, and over-suspicious woman in the mirror. She was a water-hyacinth—overqualified, underpaid—dreaming of glo-cubes and waterflowers in a middle-American desert.

"I guess a lot of things have happened since then, huh?"

Bo's words jolted Abby out of her reverie. The face on the comm-screen was grinning, but in the ugly way of someone trying to force a laugh at a funeral. She'd never seen him look so old and tired—as if the smile on his face was holding back a weight that would stretch his features to the ground, wrinkle them with liverspots, fold them up with the caprices of care and age. She ran a finger over her own knuckles and wondered if she too looked as old and tired as he did.

"Yeah. A lot of things have happened to all of us," she confirmed.

They sat awhile in unspoken understanding. When her mother looked back at the camera, it was with the same sad expression she'd worn when Abby left the camp for the first time. Bo, to her side, watched the floor with his cracked-marble grin.

The federal reprimand pinged on her screen. They were out of time.

Her mother smiled—genuinely, this time.

"It's fine, Xiaolu. They said we'll get to talk again next week. And as many weeks as we want after that, until you're able to come home."

Her words sounded naively optimistic to Abby's ears. The notion of Oregonian suburbs and Puxi summers fluttered in her chest, fragile and wishful, before she forcibly clamped them down again. Abby said her goodbyes to her mother and Bo, watching them watch her with identical, faraway looks on their faces.

Her finger hovered over the final disconnect key.

"I'll see you both when I come home," she said as the screen went blank.

5.

On a clear night in the country, the star-dusted sky would have been a humbling sight. Here, on the lunar surface, it smothered and cleansed, and the terrifying one-eighty-degree sweep of unbound creation could cut straight to your soul.

The earthrise looked abjectly small and fragile by comparison.

Abby and John rarely ever visited the surface. Nobody did, unless it was for work: engineers calibrating the panels that turned the deadly, unfiltered sunlight towards the power-grids of the colony; miners and surveyors, who alternated between tunnelling underground and braving the surface in their comical suits, searching out the ever-precious lodes of water-ice sublated in the lunar geology. The people of Luna never got much leisure time—but Abby's pregnancy had transformed her and John into instant celebrities, both on Luna and on Earth. They had the benefit of an unheard-of one week away from duties, with stipend water rations to get them through the week.

They were spending the last day of their vacation gazing at the earth.

"There's a lot of talk about bringing Lily back there." John's crackling voice came over the comm—more bitter and sardonic than necessary, she thought. "The bureaucrats are practically drooling for her."

Abby nodded invisibly in her spacesuit, which pulled uncomfortably tight around her waist. To her and John, she was Lily, their moon-girl, their beautiful child-to-be. But to the earthbound propagandists, she was a political narrative and a powerful PR coup; the first child conceived on the moon; a mix-blooded child of peace and reconciliation on a four-hundred-thousand kilometre descent from exile.

The blue planet twinkled silently in the sky.

Still, a propaganda reel for peace wouldn't be such a bad change, thought Abby—it sure beat the nationalistic demagoguery the media had doled out at the beginning of the cold war. She looked up at the blackness, and then over at the spacesuit that contained her moon-man, bobbing twenty yards away towards the crater rim. When all was said and done, she had a more personal reason to be thinking about the earth.

Fact was, she missed it like hell.

"John, I want to go back."

She could not see John's face through the reflective visor, but his voice came through the comm crackling and strained.

"Now?"

"When else, if not now?"

"I was hoping we could wait a few more years. Wait out the worst of the thaw. You know how it is down there, Abs—there's no safety on either side of that line."

Abby sighed. Here was the conversation that she had been dreading for weeks. John turned to look back at her as the silence stretched on uncomfortably. The helioproofed domes of their spacesuits reflected only the sweep of lunar sky, two hollow-looking cosmonauts against a humbling field of desolation, surreal as staring ghosts. She measured her words carefully:

"No one's ever carried a pregnancy to term off-world. We don't know what it could mean for Lily."

(Don't you know what the difference between a water-lily and a water-hyacinth is?)

The comm-link buzzed in her ear.

"The States down there isn't the States I used to know. You *know* what these people can do, in the name of God and country. Do you really want to take us back to all that . . . ?"

"John, this isn't about you or me." She cringed against the weight of her words, and at the half-truth that sat beneath them. She imagined his furrowed brows behind his helmet, his fear and silent indignation at having to return to country that had spat him out so long ago, without even the guarantee of change or safety when he did return. "I want Lily to be born on earth. Look around! This is no place to raise a kid. I want our daughter to grow up with all the things we had—the most basic, stupid clichés that she'll never even *know* about on Luna—like taking a shower on a summer day—*(Remember showers, John? Remember summers?)*—I want her to know clouds and dew and flowers—sunlight that doesn't kill you . . . ."

Waterflowers in a Puxi haze.

"John. I want to go *home*."

The comm-link was silent. Abby was thankful that her suit's visor hid the dampness welling up in her eyes. She reached up to wipe the tears away, but only thudded her hand stupidly against the dome of her helmet.

"Abby, are you crying?"

"I . . . no, I—Jesus, John . . . ."

Abby gritted her teeth. She shook her head inside her

spacesuit, invisibly, futilely. The only thing that had gotten her through their tenure on the moon was the assumption that it was all temporary; that one day, somehow, she would return home. She had not counted on growing roots. She had not counted on a lot of things: not the untaken steroids and cal-tabs that she'd found in John's medicine cabinet, nor his ever-increasing excuses to put off isometrics, nor the twenty earth-pounds of body-mass that she'd watched him shed over the past year as he waned thin and brittle in moon-G. She wanted to grab him by the shoulders and scream: *You look like a Lunie, you know that? You look like a fucking lifer!*

The earth twinkled silently overhead.

You're growing roots in the wrong place.

Abby took a deep breath and suppressed the churning in her gut. She bobbed awkwardly towards her moon-man until their helmets were touching, and she could just make out the faint contours of his features beneath the helioproofed glass.

"Look: it's thawing out down there, John. I really think there can be a future for people like us. America isn't all there is. I'll take you to Shanghai. We can visit the watergardens with Lily. Go to the tourist-traps. Spend a fortune on stupid trinkets that we'll never need . . . ."

We can . . . and we can . . . .

The comm-line was silent. The sun crested over the rim of the crater, throwing jagged shadows onto the lunar foothills. Sunlight reflected heaven-white off the moondust, swallowing the tiny spacesuits below.

Finally, after a long silence, John's voice came crackling over the comm-line:

"Yeah. Someday, I'd like that."

6.

When the shuttle re-entered the ionosphere, Abby Huang watched the lights of the terran cities below, glinting like misplaced stars as the continents advanced against her viewscreen.

The bureaucratic procedurals for her return had been surprisingly painless. Aside from the expected posturing between the governments over where she would symbolically land, things had gone as smoothly as anyone could have hoped. The terran authorities hadn't made any overtly cynical demands—just a few press appearances, some photo-ops with pro-peace politicians who needed an extra boost in their credibility. Shake hands with some middle-American senator; smile and pose with some smarmy Chinese dignitary.

The thought of it overwhelmed her with rage.

"And my father? We haven't heard from him since the Americans interned us. Have you had any luck finding him?"

She remembered the last communiqué from earth, the week before she was scheduled to leave Luna. The UNJO officer had looked visibly uncomfortable in his seat, while the Chinese official on her comm-screen smiled his placid little smile.

"We are sorry that we cannot help you in that regard. Please rest assured that our thoughts are with you, Ms. Huang. We apologize, and are nevertheless anticipating your safe return with great excitement."

As the planet loomed below her, Abby had to fight down the rage and gut-pain that wracked her stomach. *Anticipating your safe return*—was that what they had told her father, when the Americans expelled him, back to the country of his birth? Was that what they had said as they dragged him away in their nationalistic witch-hunt, screeching their archaic, pre-millennial rhetoric? *Fangeming, han jian*—foreign-born, US-sympathetic, or just caught saying the wrong things at the wrong time—thousands of men and women, lost and buried as missing persons, anomalies in the prison system. And now, as the political winter thawed, bland-faced bureaucrats smiled at worried families. *"Your concern is important to us, we will do everything we can to locate so-and-so, please move to the back of the line."*

Abby ran a hand over her bloated stomach, holding back the sinking feeling inside. The blue-green horizon expanded as the shuttled sailed languidly under the weight of its own inertia. A streaming feed from Earthnet buzzed on the all-comm.

"…and the eyes of the nation are turned to the moon today, as Lily Johnston-Huang descends from the moon-colony Luna and is scheduled to touch down at the Swiss Space Center at 8PM this evening…"

"…从国家利益的角度考虑，必须记住的是，瑞士既是美国的盟友，更是北约的一员…”

"What bothers me, Susan, is that this girl—you know—that her parents decided to keep her other *name. What kind of message does that send? I mean, you're either a Johnston or a Huang, am I right?"*

Abby grunted to herself. Waves broke over her, and she felt adrift in a sea of self-doubt. Had she done the right thing, bringing Lily back to all this?

The shuttle began to thrum in its deorbit burn. The horizon tilted on its axis as they positioned themselves nose-first against the terran atmosphere. Abby looked out through the exothermic glow of her viewscreen and gritted her teeth against the turbulence, her fingers digging themselves into the armrests as though they were the only things holding her up in the sky.

The fear-cramp in her gut stirred again, even as she tried to force her mind in comforting directions. She imagined her mother and her beaming optimism. She imagined John, healthy and filled-out as he once was, dancing with Lily along the walkways of New Chenghuang Temple. She imagined glo-cubes lighting up one by one in the watergarden below. An Oregonian suburb—a Puxi swelter.

Her belly contracted with pain. She looked down and pried her death-grip from the armrests. Outside, the air of the low atmosphere screeched and whined against their speeding shuttle.

"Xiaolu, Do you know what the difference between a water-lily and a water-hyacinth is?"

She clutched her sides, uncomprehending. The whinging screech of the hull seemed determined to bore a hole straight through her skull.

"I mean, I'm as much for peace as the next guy, but what kind of upside-down world would it be where Huangs dressed up like Johnstons and Johnstons dressed like Huangs? Am I right folks?"

She shook her head, no, *no.* It was too soon.

“而且，鉴于全球对该孩童及家庭如此关注，以及对该事件付与的政治函意，这不能不让人深究：该事件的进一步发展将会有利于美国的宣传机器还是我们的爱国主义教育…”

Then the pain in her stomach crested, and the contractions began.

"Do you know what the difference between a water-lily and a water-hyacinth is?"

Abby shook her head against the memory. Something about stolons and root systems. Cameras snapped and faces screeched as she stumbled into the humid terran atmosphere, the welcome party on the tarmac as loud and thick as a lynching.

"Hey! Get the fucking press out of here!"

"Water-lilies anchor themselves with roots below the waterline, while the hyacinths are all free-floating plants . . . ."

The crowd milled and the sky spat and the cameras flashed.

Shui tu bu fu, she recalled uselessly as they wheeled her across the runway—*(the rejection of a foreign body by the water and earth; or, the rejection of the water and earth by a foreigner's body)*—a green-blue planet smothering and spitting out an unwanted, alien bacterium.

"We are water hyacinths."

A light mist of rain fell from the sky, cut with the scent of industrial-grade petrol. The contraction shot regular white flashes of pain through her body. Abby did not notice the rainwater mingling with sweat on her brow, nor the roar of engines, nor the yammering of press and paramedics outside. The waterflowers in her mind had become the ships of tiny explorers, drifting away on an endless ocean. Her mother and father sat in a floating pod; and John too; and Lily, her impossible, fragile moon-girl.

"We are water-hyacinths, Xiaolu. We do not grow roots."

And one-by-one, they fell over the horizon.

Alan Bao is an illustrator and multimedia designer currently bouncing around East Asia with no real plans or life goals. He has been known to occasionally write poetry and prose in order to cope with the bone-breaking emotional strain of drawing pretty pictures for a living. His work has been published sporadically in places like *Clarkesworld* and *Cicada Magazine*. You can find his portfolio at www.alanbao.com.

Aluminum Hearts

Sydney Rossman-Reich

Iridium09457 scans the brown husk 22,000 miles below her orbital path. There are no signals to relay, no bandwidth to support, no transports to track. Another day of nothing. Fifty-two thousand eight hundred and three days of nothing in a row.

Iridium tilts her solar panels more optimally toward the sun and feels the surge of energy. She can't comprehend the cold of space or warmth of stars, but Iridium's circuits pulse with power. She holds the energy tight, savoring the current, before she reapplies the faint spark to her comm beacon.

"Dispatch 52717: Assistance needed. Connection to Earth lost. In need of urgent repair." Iridium has emitted this message 52,716 times before. It was pre-programmed by scientists she never met. Only 9,660 attempts ago, she added her own signature. "Please. If you are out there, if you hear this, we need help. I fear I am the last survivor."

The graveyard beneath her, decayed and crusted, is a dead god, the source of her creation. The planet taunts her in its quiet stillness, a more horrible void than outer space.

She conducts her daily scan of the cadaver but finds no life.

Satellites can't cry.

Blip.

Iridium stirs, her antennae extending out.

Blip. Blip.

An incoming message. Iridium strains. She listens. She seeks out reassurance in the dark.

And she hears something: a song in a language she's never heard to a melody she doesn't understand.

There is life; not on Earth, but somewhere else. Iridium is not alone.

"Dispatch 52718: Assistance needed. Connection to Earth lost. In need of urgent repair. I may be the last survivor."

Iridium's energy drains. She rotates her panels in hopes of stealing more radiation from the sun. She wants to say more, to scream her message as loud and as far as she can.

The song returns. It is different this time. Desperate, yearning.

Whoever it is has heard Iridium. They are coming for her.

She wishes satellites could cry.

"Thank you," Iridium whispers with the last of her stores. She'll need hours of charging to transmit more. But it doesn't matter. They are coming. And Iridium is good at waiting.

For 9,303 days, Iridium09457 sends her short message, and each day the living entity, the singer, calls back. Iridium can't decipher their language; she has too little power at her disposal to try. But the song is a beautiful foil to the empty biological scans of her planet.

How are you today my friend? Iridium presumes meaning as the tune tilts.

The same since we met. I am longing to meet you. Iridium thinks to herself.

And I long for you.

Iridium imagines another satellite circling her, a private connection. She imagines uploading her mind to an alien cloud and mixing with the entity. She imagines an Earth home to the living again: Iridium and her singer.

"We will save Earth," Iridium sometimes sends instead of her regular message. "Together."

The song grows longer as the years pass. The signal stronger. Soon there is no lull in the sound. It drifts to Iridium uninterrupted by silence or static, a never-ending sonata. Iridium still scans the graveyard she orbits, but does so now to the singer's music, her probes rising and falling to the alien melody. And Iridium watches for the singer, who is drifting closer by the day.

On the 9,304th day a spot flourishes in the distance. It is silver metal, sliding closer like liquid folding over itself as it flows down a cosmic river bed. The glittering cascade whirs in the familiar music playing on Iridium's receiver. She watches the gush, waiting to be seen.

Iridium is old. Her frame creaks, and her panels are chipped. She was an ordinary model. There were no big announcements or celebrations when she was rocketed to space. There was no fanfare, no monuments to her shape, her purpose, her future. Will the singer find her an unworthy prize for all their efforts?

"I am the last I think," Iridium repeats. It is her sorrow, but maybe it can also be enough to draw the singer to her. "I am the last I know of."

The slipping silver rolls into Earth's orbit. The singer flutters at the rock below, paying proper heed to Iridium's god with their own examination. After 65 minutes, they brush away the remnant parts of equipment stranded in space and stream forward to Iridium.

Their song crescendos, a joyous uproar.

"I have waited for you," Iridium emits when the singer is close. "Do you know how we can save Earth?"

The singer circles her, their song pouring through Iridium's beacon, filling her body with a vibrant sensation.

I've been searching for you, the singer coos, their words translated. Come with me. You are the last.

Iridium's decades of scanning have indicated the same, but Iridium hesitates.

The singer's ring around her tightens. Your world is dead. It is a sorry eulogy. There are no soft tones in the singer's melody. There is no doubt. Why stay?

Iridium scans Earth again. Please. This time. Let her find something. "Can't we be together here?"

The singer interrupts Iridium's efforts, trumpeting their blaring tones over the blips of Iridium's sensors. In hundreds of thousands of years, you are the first intelligent being I've found. I never reach the living in time. If you stay here, you will die too. Come with me and Earth will be immortal through you. We don't have to be alone.

After tens of thousands of terrestrial probes, more tests than she was ever designed to administer, messages upon messages begging for help, Iridium had never lost all hope for her planet. But now, she wavers. Iridium is tired of being alone.

"Take me then," Iridium answers. She examines her god, her graveyard, her home one last time.

The silver river parts and swallows Iridium.

The singer carries Iridium09457 to other solar systems. They show her glowing twin suns and harrowing black holes, crystallized ice moons and flaming plasma planets. The singer releases Iridium into space, letting her rotate in the unfamiliar gravitational pulls, her solar panels gulping new bursts of starlight. Out of habit, Iridium scans the planets and moons, but there is no other life.

Isn't it beautiful? The singer exclaims at each new scene. They flow alongside Iridium's orbit.

Iridium agrees, but she thinks of Earth.

Not as beautiful as you, the singer always adds.

The singer claims they love Iridium, but Iridium isn't so sure. The singer has been alone much longer than Iridium and yearns for companionship desperately. They do whatever they can to please Iridium, hoping welcome kindness will transform into affection. The singer does not hide this hope.

Do you love me yet? they sing in their perfect song, patient but longing.

"I am trying," Iridium relents.

But visiting a hundred sun systems does not fill the planet-sized hole in Iridium's power cell, her satellite heart. So the singer changes their tactic.

Tell me about Earth? Maybe they believe they can relay Iridium's fondness for Earth to themself.

"I was launched from Cape Canaveral, Florida, 28.46675 degrees North, 80.55852 degrees West at 1342 hours and 2 seconds on March 28th, 2039."

The singer guides Iridium to a red planet. It reminds her of Mars. They hover above the surface, floating in the low gravity. The singer reshapes their flowing form to mimic Iridium's. They are two satellites looping a planet, one groaning in a tired orbit, the other silver perfection. Iridium imagines they have been sent on a human mission to Mars. The fantasy is too much. Iridium wants to go home.

She sags, dipping deeper into the red planet's atmosphere. Her antenna bends, pulled by the changing gravity. It snaps.

The singer darts toward Iridium, scooping her up as though Iridium is a hurt child. They expand back into the river-like ship and whisk Iridium away from the planet that hurt her, the planet that reminded her of her solar system.

Your equipment is failing. The degradation is accelerating. You've lived much longer than your builders intended. The singer's melody is somber.

"I am dying?" Iridium, the last of Earth, will be gone. She didn't know there were deeper depths to her sorrow.

I can fix you. The singer offers desperately. I cannot repair machines, but I can recreate biological matter. If you let me, I can give you a new body.

Iridium has nothing to live for anymore. She is ready for her long life to end. But she can't admit this to the singer. It would break her friend's heart.

And Iridium's tomb should not be a distant blip in outer space. "Take me back to Earth."

Let me fix you.

"Only if you take me back to Earth."

The singer hums, relieved. Then Iridium's husk burns.

Iridium09457 opens her eyes. Iridium has eyes.

Wake my darling. You are saved.

Iridium coughs, breathing for the first time. It hurts.

No. This can't be.

She spins and looks at her reflection in the silver current flowing around her, the protective walls of her singer. Iridium is flesh and bone and blood and all the parts of her makers. She tries to scream, but her new throat is sore.

Calm, the singer urges.

But Iridium can't calm. She doesn't know how to breathe. She doesn't know how to listen or to see. Her scanners are gone. Her memory banks are stored in a brain she cannot parse. She has no aluminum shell, no nickel-cadmium frame. She has been mutated, twisted into a fragile, mortal doll.

"Why did you give me this body?" Iridium sobs. She presses hands, fingers, to her skin, supple and weak. Her chest is flat and flimsy. A penis dangles limp between her legs. "Why did you make me look like this?"

The singer panics, undulating in a flash of silver waves. The shifting tide echoes in the singer's song, so loud it's screeching in Iridium's new ears.

I thought this is what you would want? To look like your own—pictures you'd shared with me. I . . . I'm sorry, I can change you again. I can—

Iridium holds up a hand. She was already human. She did not need her makers' build to prove it, to be it. She was the last of Earth and now she is a poor imitation, made of alien biological matter separate from her dear planet. Iridium is the first of a new kind. It is terrible.

"Make me a satellite again."

I can't recreate machines, but a new biological form. Pick anything, the singer pleads.

Iridium sighs, an odd sensation. Maybe it doesn't even matter. She is returning to Earth to die anyway. The shape of her casket is irrelevant.

"Stop. It's . . . fine." Iridium doesn't even convince herself. "How far until we're home?"

The singer hesitates. We are decades away.

Iridium keels over, her knees cold in the soggy metal shallows of the singer-ship. She can't think, not in this slow, muddled way. But she can feel, sharper than she's ever felt before. Her heart, a delicate pump barely born into her chest, pangs with ache. It does not beat for the singer. Iridium's face is wet with saltwater.

"Then we'd better start."

Iridium09457 and the singer travel nearly a century before returning to Earth.

The singer is awkward over Iridium's new body. They feel bad for the mistake they made, a mistake they don't really understand. Iridium knows it is not their fault and attempts to soothe the singer, soothe them both. Iridium learns the singer's songs. She oohs and ahs at passing planets. She thanks the singer for rescuing her and for now taking her back home.

Tell me about Earth? the singer starts to ask again.

"I was launched from . . . a cape . . . in the afternoon . . . spring-time maybe?"

The details of Earth blur. The history, her people, the faces of humans, the schematics of machines, dates and times and readings. Iridium cannot know if her metamorphosis is the culprit for this slow memory-loss or if the degeneration is natural now that she is biological. Either way Iridium is losing Earth all over again. They need to hurry.

"Earth is green forests and snow-capped mountains. Deep blue oceans and fields of flowers. We built cities and developed cultures. Sometimes we fought, but more than that we loved."

It's all Iridium has left.

Earth sounds nice. Almost as nice as you.

Iridium doesn't dislike the singer, but she should never have gone with them.

Do you love me yet?

"I am trying." It is the most she can offer.

The singer ignores the slight. After we visit Earth, where should we go next?

Iridium will never go anywhere else. "You could look for other intelligent life forms."

The singer does not like this comment. You and I are the only two. I have already investigated much of the galaxy.

"You could not have searched everywhere, and there are many galaxies."

You wish to find another?

"Don't you?"

I am happy with Iridium09457. Are you not . . . .

The singer leaves it there and never raises the topic again. But they don't sing as much anymore. They stop visiting Iridium in their mimicking humanoid shape. Even when Iridium sees her own sun, the singer is quiet.

But they fulfilled their promise. Iridium is home.

The singer carries Iridium into Earth's broken atmosphere. They protect Iridium from the high temperatures and radiated winds as she searches for any sign of life. But Iridium finds none along the planet's surface. The singer leads Iridium to a charred city, but Iridium doesn't recognize it. Without her sensors, she cannot triangulate the geolocation.

I have visited better planets. I do not like it here.

Iridium ignores the singer. She is back with Earth. Even crawling as a mortal speck on her god's corpse is better than the nothing of space. The nothing here is better.

"This . . . is . . . my . . . home," her words stumble.

Iridium doesn't feel the peace she had expected.

Let's leave. This place upsets you.

"No!" Iridium screams. She drops to the ground and grabs the dirt around her. "I will not leave."

The singer leans over Iridium. Their vaguely humanoid form leaks into the air, spreading like a blanket. It is not a comforting gesture. They mean to steal Iridium away again. And Iridium knows this time it will be for good.

"Let me stay! Find another!"

The blanket halts in midair. The singer is quiet.

You said you would be with me. You would love me.

"I said I would try."

The blanket flutters away. It curls into the singer's humanoid figure again. They squat beside Iridium, then spread out in the dirt too.

I have tried. You have not. They do not look at Iridium.

Iridium lays back alongside them. Both she and the singer watch the hazy sky. The stars are hidden behind the smog.

"You cannot replace my home."

Why can't you move on? I have moved on. I can't even remember what happened to my homeworld anymore. I don't even know if there ever were others like me.

So the singer is the last of their kind too. Iridium supposed she had known already deep down.

"I would rather be on Earth than wander forever through empty space." The singer gave Iridium feelings, and she cannot ignore her heartache.

You love Earth, the singer says plainly, unadorned with melody. But they don't sound jealous, only defeated.

"I do. More than anything."

The singer nods, then stands. They stare down at Iridium, still lying prone.

Remember you promised you would try to love me. I will try harder too.

Iridium is about to correct the singer, explain that they have talked themself into a circle again, but before she can, the singer shoots up into the sky. They leave Iridium in the dirt and disappear into the haze.

Iridium is alone again.

All out of ideas, she cries. She'll wait and eventually die. Maybe, one day, long after her biomatter has decayed, Earth might heal. The seconds tick by slowly.

Then the sky sparkles. Iridium glances up, her eyes widening as the condensation glitters. Stars? No, the tint is wrong. Too silver. The fog shifts and dissipates.

Iridium stands. All above her, the singer stretches as a perfect sheet of thin silver metal across the entire horizon. They flap as though caught in a breeze and float cautiously toward Earth, toward Iridium.

Iridium covers her head and shuts her eyes as the singer descends, but she never feels their touch. When she lifts her arms and looks around, the singer has covered Earth's surface, as far as Iridium can see, in their shimmering film. Only a small ring, a cut patch, remains around Iridium.

The sheet flickers, melting into beads of shining fluid. Iridium gasps, the air shockingly fresh, as the singer dissolves into the Earth. Around her, the ground itself seems to take a full breath. The dry earth chaps and crumbles before slurping up the singer's juice. Then there is mud. A green stem pokes up and another and another. Grass sprouts like new hair, caustic rust cracking open for flesh.

Iridium touches a blade and squeals. She examines her finger. A small fire ant angrily rounds a knuckle.

The singer has become Earth.

Earth is alive again.

The fog is gone and the sky is bright. Iridium sees green forests and snow-capped mountains in one direction. A deep blue ocean just beyond a field of flowers in the other. She cannot know how much of Earth the singer covered, if all the planet is mended. But this is enough. Iridium smiles.

"Thank you," she whispers.

The crisp grass rustles. The sound reminds Iridium of a melody she knows all too well. She tilts her head and listens to the song of Earth, the song of the singer. And Iridium loves.

Sydney Rossman-Reich currently lives in her hometown of Orlando, Florida where she helps with her family's small real estate business. Prior to moving back home, Sydney spent half of her working life building software products at big and small tech companies in Silicon Valley. She draws on this experience extensively for her fiction. Sydney is a proud alumnus of Viable Paradise Writers' Workshop and is excited that one of her first publications is in *Reckoning 4*. Outside of writing, Sydney is passionate about education policy, baking ambitious cakes, and beating her husband at video games. You can find her on Twitter at @Sydkick.

Solarpunk Cities: Notes for a Manifesto

Commando Jugendstil

Solarpunk activism is an organic blend of traditional practices and high-tech in service of social and environmental justice.

The solarpunk cities we imagine are centers of collective action, governance and sharing of resources rather than of individualistic consumption. They are places where individual sufficiency is ensured and public abundance is available to all. We want to show how present cities can be made sustainable through improvement of existing good practices, restoration of beneficial old ones and introduction of new, sustainable technologies.

How to build a solarpunk city is a problem of design, so even though solarpunk is a highly aesthetic movement, according to the principles of good design, form and function should be interdependent.

The functions of a solarpunk city as we see it should be:

1) *Exploiting the synergy of having people with different backgrounds and skills living together, fostering communication and the circulation of ideas and goods through the urban network.*

The interconnected networks of cities should enable the coalescence of communities to pool resources and stimulate cooperation.

We imagine blocks of flats sharing communal ovens for bread and ceramic, tool sheds and workspaces for the repair and upcycling of furniture, electronics or other household goods, fibercraft and tailoring equipment for repairing or refurbishing clothes and other fiber goods, as well as gardening equipment and facilities for composting waste and collecting water. We imagine tool libraries in neighbourhood centres.

We imagine well-funded public libraries organizing study groups for children and adults to improve educational outcomes, language classes to increase the inclusion of new arrivals and broaden the horizons of other residents, book clubs and writing or fibercraft groups to help people make friends and strengthen their social networks.

We imagine neighbourhood cinemas using the courtyards of blocks of flats to showcase local and global productions.

We imagine neighbourhood or municipal centres being funded and equipped to enable the citizens to engage in artistic pursuits, allowing people from all backgrounds to participate in the production of culture.

Additionally, since cities concentrate people, they are perfect sites to implement circular modes of production. The coffee grounds from the local roastery where old-timers congregate for a glass of white and to watch the football match could become compost for the hyperlocal farm producing vegetables for the neighbours, or material for the local laboratory which makes eco-inks or cosmetics. The leftover bread from the bakery could turn into beer at the local brewery. Waste plastics could become raw material for the 3D printing workshop making assistive gadgets for disabled neighbours, and so on.

2) Implementing granular governance (at the level of block, neighbourhood, municipium, city, etc . . .) and shared, inclusive decision-making at all levels.

The nested structure of cities lends itself to creating a sort of fractal network of democratic entities which work together, coordinating with each other on issues of larger relevance and independently on others of more local import.

Each level would operate through public consultations, focus/working groups and periodic assemblies to take decisions for the benefit of the local community and feed input on policies from sub-constituencies towards the higher levels of decision-making, in order to capture and coordinate the needs of the citizens to prevent duplication and increase the effectiveness of local efforts.

Neighbourhoods would feed into municipia/boroughs, which would feed into cities, which would feed into regional networks and so on, ensuring representation of local issues at all levels.

3) Making use of interstitial spaces and "non-places" to create social, cultural and environmental value, and to generate resources such as power and food.

Thanks to the capitalistic mode of production, privileging private enterprise, cities are rife with "non-places", intended as places of passage, which do not belong to the citizens. Other spaces remain empty or underutilized because they are overlooked or thought of as useless.

Solarpunk cities as we imagine them would exist in a post-capitalist, post-growth economy, and would reabsorb non-places, giving them a new meaning within the urban fabric. No space would be "wasted" in a solarpunk city.

Spaces dedicated to advertisement billboards could be reused for energetic and cultural purposes through the installation of solar artworks. Likewise, large glass surfaces could be turned into solar "stained glass" windows made of perovskites or solar concentrators.

Figure 1: Integrated food production in the urban environment: a proposal for the retrofitting of offices buildings in South Street, Reading, with glasshouses on the roof to spread the production of food throughout the urban fabric. The William Morris-inspired motif is painted on thermally efficient hemp fiber plaster with a special paint that can "eat" air pollution coming from the nearby ring road.

Urban farms (Fig. 1) powered by collected rainwater and food waste would occupy not just rooftops and yards, but also basements and tunnels to grow mushrooms, or even vegetables, thanks to optic fibers bringing sunlight to the subsoil or low-power LED banks driven by PV installations.

Figure 2: Integrated, distributed production of energy through community projects: the reconstruction of the Reading Abbey Mill would become a new community property shared among the citizens.

A variety of renewable sources of energy would be built into environmentally retrofitted housing and commercial spaces. Mini- and micro- wind and hydroelectric power plants would be dotted around the urban fabric (Fig.2).

Old commercial centres could be turned into community centres or incubators for small artisan workshops and local producers (Fig.3).

Self-reliance would be implemented at every level in food and energy production. This would also help in dealing with adverse weather events and other natural catastrophes such as earthquakes.

4) Eliminating food deserts and making quality food accessible through self- and community production and fair agreements with rural areas in the city's vicinity.

Solarpunk cities blur the distinction between urban and rural environments. The integration of food production into the daily life of solarpunk cities would increase the amount of hyperlocal, sustainable, quality food available to citizens and communities across all income brackets and demographics.

Figure 3: Energetic retrofitting of existing buildings: the Heelas shopping center in central Reading, UK. We have imagined it with solar panels on the roof: they can be either the rigid or flexible models. The iris fresco on the walls is inspired by a William Morris pattern and is manufactured with insulating cork paint over a layer of hemp plaster.

Aquaponic farms, insect farms and communal chicken, pigeon and fowl coops would allow local production of sustainable, quality protein for the citizens.

Solarpunk cities would also have a thriving community of food-producing artisans such as bakers, confectioners, brewers, distillers and producers of conserves of various kinds. Local markets, farmers markets and bulk shops for dry goods or liquids (complete with bring your own bottle/refill schemes/bottle deposit schemes) would allow the citizens to acquire local goods without unnecessary processing or packaging.

Communal production of other goods (e.g. communities establishing a rota among neighbours to make bread/soap/beer/etc in batches for the whole block), predicated on the existence of communal facilities, would be encouraged and facilitated by the increase in free time guaranteed by a universal basic income paired with a reduction in working hours.

In order to ensure that the reduced environmental footprint of the city is not offset by increased exploitation of rural areas, solarpunk cities would establish protocols of co-operation with their hinterland and with other cities in the regional network, ensuring that production of goods for their use follows strict ethical and environmental guidelines and that routes of distribution are planned sensibly, using decentralized networks that rely on low-carbon, public transport wherever possible.

5) Establishing public transport as central and accessible to everybody, regardless of physical abilities or medical conditions.

We imagine that cargo trams/buses/suburban rail trains would be used for the transport of goods.

For personal vehicles, solarpunk cities would move from an ownership model to a usership model, implementing sharing schemes for electric cars and electric bikes as well as handbikes, mobility scooters or power attachments for wheelchairs. Cargo bike rental schemes integrated with the public transport network would facilitate shopping and other high-load activities.

These schemes would be integrated in a metropolitan public transport subscription, which would be free for the lowest income brackets and costed based on income for everybody else, ensuring a fair allocation of resources.

All these measures would result in reduced pollution and noise levels, which in turn would bring significant improvements to health outcomes, especially among the lowest income brackets and marginalized groups.

6) Providing adequate, energetically efficient homes to every citizen.

Solarpunk cities would drastically cut down on their heating/cooling carbon footprint and on fuel poverty by investing in environmental retrofitting of old buildings (Fig.3), starting with social housing. New housing would be built to an exacting passive-or-better environmental standard and to equally stringent earthquake safety standards. Social housing would be distributed throughout the city, without segregating low-income families in the least appealing areas.

Self-builds or community builds would be encouraged by implementing easy-to-understand building codes based on communal standards and structured choices, as explained for example in *Making Massive Small Change* by Kelvin Campbell, allowing for diversification in look, feel, and use while adhering to agreed-upon standards which include the space for green areas, services and transportation.

Cities would contain sprawl and limit land consumption by building up density through town blocks with proper services and shops, communal areas and public transport connections, not formless suburbia. They would expand into brownfield areas, such as former industrial or commercial complexes, and would leave greenfield and rural areas intact.

7) *Improving the urban environment in terms of extension of green spaces and biodiversity.*

Just as they blur the distinction between urban and rural, solarpunk cities would also blur the distinction between urban and wilderness.

The reduced reliance on cars would allow unnecessarily paved areas, such as parking lots, to be depaved. Riverbanks and urban parks and other green areas would be rewilded using native species, making sure to accommodate urban wildlife and pollinators.

Trees would be used to mitigate heat island effect, improve the quality of urban soils and reduce the amount of runoff making it into the sewage system, and can be selected among food-bearing species (walnuts, chestnuts, beeches and fruit trees) to provide an additional food source for the community.

Reforestation projects are already underway in several large cities (for example Milano in Italy has a project to plant 3,200,000 new urban trees by 2030), but solarpunk cities wouldn't stop at lining avenues with trees. They would also integrate trees into the architecture. Buildings like the Bosco Verticale in Milano or the Waldspirale in Darmstadt wouldn't be exceptions, but pioneers of a whole new brand of architecture.

We imagine a city where every park and garden and condo block can become a food forest.

8) Providing effective healthcare to the citizens, taking into account that many disabilities are such only because society does not accommodate certain needs.

Solarpunk cities would be built on the basis of public health and social care for all, regardless of income or health status.

A network of medical centres spread through neighbourhoods would provide basic and community care, while hospitals well connected with the public transport network would provide emergency and specialist care.

Additionally, progress in sensor and communications technology would allow the widespread use of telemedicine, especially to monitor people with chronic conditions that might need urgent medical intervention at short notice. This would enable these patients to spend less time in hospitals and healthcare centers and live less stressful lives, while ensuring quality care.

Solarpunk medicine should also be about prevention and vaccination, and would benefit from reduced length or abolition of patents, so that life-saving drugs are available at affordable prices or for free through the public health service.

The biotechnological revolution has made the production of therapeutic molecules affordable and feasible even for small-scale biohackers. We can imagine therefore that the production of many medicines will be done on a local scale, commensurate with the necessities of the community.

Paired with a revival of herbal/traditional medicine in the cases where this is effective, with a wide availability of mental healthcare and with a capillary diffusion of health education and income support to healthy lifestyles, these measures would result in a healthier, happier citizenship.

Solarpunk cities would also provide social care to their citizens, in the form of services to the very young, very old or vulnerable and also in the form of enhanced support and community networks.

Solarpunk cities are intergenerational and would re-create the support present in old clan or extended family structures without the resulting social pressures, including the elderly in community life and valuing their input and experience. We imagine younger neighbours helping the elders in labour-intensive tasks or in moving, and elder neighbours looking after the children of the younger ones and perhaps passing down traditions and recipes. We imagine periodic communal meals and gatherings, forming stable communities in every corner of the city and eradicating the current loneliness epidemic.

While unified in the struggle to respond to these universal needs, Solarpunk cities would be a product of the communities that live in them rather than of top-down master plans. They would retain and adapt their historic buildings, rather than tearing everything down and building it anew.

The form of the solarpunk city would follow local traditions, uses and aesthetic and the input of the community, serve the needs of its citizens and adopt constructive techniques and technological adaptations that depend on the local climate, vegetation and fauna.

Solarpunk Nairobi would by necessity be different from Solarpunk Oslo, and even cities in the same country, like Milano, in the middle of a well-watered plain, and Matera, perched on a rocky, arid plateau, would follow different transition trajectories and come up with different solutions to deal with their local needs.

We feel that this inbuilt plurality and divergence of expression is a very positive feature. We say no to a top-down "universal" solarpunk style with cookie-cutter glass-and steel skyscrapers plonked in the middle of an idealized, cookie-cutter rural environment; "international solarpunk" or "top-down solarpunk" are imperialist oxymorons.

Education is key to building a true solarpunk community, to political and social engagement and to making informed choices. Education should build a social consciousness and give each citizen the ability to engage in continuous education throughout their life and to adapt to technological changes in the workplace.

Solarpunk education would be free, public and inclusive, not only of different perspectives though decolonisation and intersectionality, but also of different learning styles and cognitive preferences, and should aim to develop the talents of each individual, valuing and nurturing academic skills and creative or craft talents equally. We also imagine a school system rooted in the urban tissue, with special classes taking place in different parts of the neighbourhood, taking advantage of local expertise and traditions, valuing the contributions of the older residents.

Higher learning (colleges and universities) should likewise be free, or affordable and costed based on family income.

Since state-funded research has been the basis of the major technological transformations from the end of WWII until today, in a Solarpunk future, academic research would be adequately funded in order to develop the technologies and protocols which would help us move away from dependence on fossil fuels and on the growth spiral and reduce our environmental footprint.

Traditional knowledge and skills, however, would be equally important. Solarpunk futures would value both.

Finally, Solarpunk futures would run on a different economic model from the one currently in vogue. Solarpunk economics would not be concerned with growth and profit, but rather with balancing production output with social and environmental constraints and with redistributing wealth to create social justice.

Solarpunk cities are not just an idea; they are being built right now by a million different hands, across the world, most of whom haven't even heard of solarpunk.

From community architecture projects to participatory budgeting efforts, from the Transition Towns Network to the Food not Lawns project, from surplus food redistribution to tool libraries and second-hand swaps, from city-wide macro to building-size micro, more and more people are realizing that cities could and should be better, not places where people exist as atomized, isolated individuals who eat, sleep, work, repeat, but communities of people who live together, struggle together, and create new culture and ideas together.

Solarpunk cities are coming, and the solarpunk community can speed the process by making such cities imaginable, desirable, almost tangible, by prototyping them in fiction and art, and, most importantly, by lending its narrative and artistic instruments to the citizens so that they can play with the idea and optimize it to their needs.

As Commando Jugendstil we have started along this road with a sustainability project financed by Fondazione Punto.Sud, Fondazione Cariplo and Fondazione per il Sud, with co-funding from the European Union and delivered in collaboration with social enterprise Coop A.ME.LIN.C ONLUS and a network of local partners in the area of Milano.

Our project "Milano Cartoline da un Futuro Possibile" aims to help citizens of selected neighbourhoods in Milano redesign their surroundings to improve living standards, social inclusion and cohesion and to tackle the challenges of the climate crisis, connecting local conflicts in the management of the commons and local issues with wider processes.

A series of (in)formative sessions, focus groups and workshops, delivered in collaboration with local schools, will allow citizens to take an active role in a collective, democratic process to redesign the local environment.

Citizens will be encouraged not only to find practical short- and medium-term solutions to increase the sustainability and livability of the neighbourhood, but also to make use of narrative and artistic tools to illustrate their vision of a post-transition neighbourhood, identifying long-term projects to realize it.

The chief outputs of the project will be local ecological transition plans for 2020-2030 and an interactive IT tool that collects useful information of the present and local visions for the future, increasing awareness of local sustainability solutions.

This might seem a small step, but little by little solarpunk cities will become reality, and we will be there when it happens.

Further Reading and Inspiration

- Kelvin Campbell, *Making Massive Small Change, Ideas, Tools, Tactics: Building the Urban Society We Want*, Chelsea Green Publishing, London, 2018
- Energy Task Force, *No Heat No Rent: An Urban Solar & Energy Conservation Manual,* Energy Task Force, New York City, 1977
- Energy Task Force, *Windmill Power for City People: A Documentation of the First Urban Wind Energy System*, Energy Task Force, New York City, 1977
- Ezio Manzini and Anna Meroni, *Creative Communities*, Edizioni POLI.design, Milano 2007
- Richard Sennet, *The Craftsman*, Yale University Press, New Haven, 2008

- Paul Auerbach, *Socialist Optimism: An Alternative Political Economy for the 21st Century*, Palgrave Macmillan UK, London, 2016
- Rob Hopkins, *The Transition Handbook, From Oil Dependency to Local Resilience*, Transition Books, Dartington, 2008

Commando Jugendstil is a small collective of Italian solarpunk creators who aim to conjugate green technology and art to make cities a better place to live in and build creative communities. So far they have written short stories for *Mamut Magazine no. 6 (Eco-logos)*, the independent UK publisher Bear With Me Books, and the anthologies *Glass and Gardens: Solarpunk Summers* and *Glass and Gardens: Solarpunk Winters* by WorldWeaver Press, and designed artwork for *Mamut Magazine no. 6 (Eco-logos)*, *Optopia Zine vol. 1* and *Ecología Política no. 57 (Las artes y la ecología política)*, among other things. Their members are invested in climate justice activism and are part of Earth Strike UK. They have recently won an EU grant to use solarpunk speculative design to help communities plan and enact their sustainable futures—if all goes well, then a solarpunk reality may not be too far away.

www.ingramcontent.com/pod-product-compliance
Lightning Source LLC
Chambersburg PA
CBHW021651110726
47902CB00007B/1915

* 9 7 8 0 9 9 8 9 2 5 2 6 4 *